FUNDING A MISSION

FUNDING A MISSION

One Donor & One Penny at A Time

*Communicating Your Mission & Building
Transformational Relationships With Donors.*

Zenebe Abebe

Funding A Mission
Copyright © 2019 by Zenebe Abebe. All rights reserved.

No part of this publication may be reproduced, stored in a retrieval system or transmitted in any way by any means, electronic, mechanical, photocopy, recording or otherwise without the prior permission of the author except as provided by USA copyright law.

The opinions expressed by the author are not necessarily those of URLink Print and Media.

1603 Capitol Ave., Suite 310 Cheyenne, Wyoming USA 82001
1-888-980-6523 | admin@urlinkpublishing.com

URLink Print and Media is committed to excellence in the publishing industry.

Book design copyright © 2019 by URLink Print and Media. All rights reserved.

Cover Photo by Gwen Gustafson-Zook

Published in the United States of America
ISBN 978-1-64367-545-9 (Paperback)
ISBN 978-1-64367-546-6 (Hardback)
ISBN 978-1-64367-547-3 (Digital)

12.09.19

> The majority of my fundraising experiences and stories expressed in this book occurred during my tenure at Mennonite Central Committee (MCC). As MCC is gearing up to celebrate 100 years of relief, development, and peace around the globe, I wish this great organization the best.

Note

MCC is a worldwide ministry of Anabaptist churches with around 1000 employees serving around the globe. MCC operates in more than 50 countries in ministries of relief, development, and peace building. In the U.S., the organization is divided into four regions: East Coast, Central States, Great Lakes and West Coast. Each region is incorporated with its own board and executive director. The Great Lakes region is made up of seven states. All references made to MCC and stories told in this book are only from the Great Lakes region in the U.S. For more about MCC's worldwide ministry, go to mcc.org.

Contents

Author's Note i
Acknowledgements v
Foreword vii
Introduction xv

Section 1
Looking Ahead and Setting the Parameters

Commitment to a Mission 3
Guiding Principles 11
Being Devoted to Your Mission 15
Historical Context 19
On-the-job Training 27
How Much Wealth Is There, and
Who Needs It the Most? 35
Preparedness 39
Looking for Generous Individuals 43
Sharing the Wealth 49
Finding Partners in Fundraising 53

Section 2
Planning and Strategizing, Staying in Touch, and Building Trust

Strategic Planning 59
Qualities and Measures of Success
in Fundraising 71
Board Involvement in Fundraising 81
Listening to Donors 89
Why People Give 97
Legacy Donors 103
First-Time Donors 113

Section 3
A Framework for Action: Showing Results and Building Trust

Developing an Organizational Plan for
Fundraising 121
Communication 125
Empowering Those Being Served 133
Endowment 139
Accountability 143

Section 4
Sharing Ideas and Words of Encouragement

A Book to Assist Fundraisers 149
Incentive to Write 155
Concluding Thoughts 161

Author's Note

This is not a how-to book. This is a book that reflects on what was, is, and can be in a nonprofit fundraising world. I do not claim to be an expert in nonprofit fundraising, but I excelled in my time spent fundraising for nonprofits. I enjoyed the experience immensely.

This book is a reflection of my own fundraising experiences, in addition to those of others, as documented through literature reviews and survey findings. It is written from my personal perspective and seeks to communicate the culture of philanthropy present in nonprofit organizations. As I write candidly, I hope my readers will find these true stories to be inspiring and helpful to them. I tried to communicate ways to match the needs of desperate people to those who are passionate and generous in order to make a difference in the lives of the needy.

I have found that existing fundraising theory is rarely based on practical documentation. To my surprise, though many of the books I reviewed focused on nonprofit fundraising,

Funding A Mission

the practitioners shared very little of their personal experiences. As such, it appears to me that the resources currently available to fundraisers are lacking. Conversely, this book shares over five years' worth of stories from my fundraising experience, stories that showcase personal relationships with donors and how enjoyable fundraising can be.

I will share the insights of executive directors of nonprofit organizations, as well as the works of scholars in the field of nonprofit fundraising. Additionally, I have compiled existing knowledge within the field of nonprofit fundraising and have included the results of a survey of current professionals, both those who have been in the field longer than I and those new to the profession.

In order to support the very premise of the book—that funding a mission really does matter—a survey was conducted. All nonprofit fundraising professionals in the study were contacted by phone to ask them to participate in the study. This phone call was followed by an email with a brief description of the purpose of the study, a timeline, and an assurance to the participants of total confidentiality.

Sixteen survey participants received 24 questions by email. We garnered a 100% response. In addition, we received 15 written comments. Not everyone that completed

Author's Note

the survey provided written comments, and several offered more than one comment.

It is important to note that the sample size for this survey might be too small to draw any significant conclusions. However, the importance of the findings is that it provides a snapshot from the perspective of individuals working in three different types of nonprofit organizations, each of which has its set of challenges and opportunities. Participants also represent domestic and international work.

It is my hope that the stories and experiences I share will be of interest to all those currently working or volunteering at nonprofits, board members, and donors, because as you give back to your communities you are also making a difference in many people's lives around the globe.

This book is organized into four main sections. The first section considers the importance of looking ahead as you plan nonprofit fundraising. The second section deals with planning and strategizing. The third section deals with the responsibility and accountability of your organization. Finally, the book ends with my thoughts and commentary on my experience in the field of philanthropy.

This book aims to help nonprofit fundraisers think boldly, approach funders with confidence, and to always act with gratitude, trust, and respect.

Donors expect an organization commit to carrying out its mission statement, so it is pivotal that we follow through with our promises. There is much to write about with regards to nonprofit fundraising. The personal stories shared by fundraisers are as diverse and unique as the people sharing them. These people's stories have the potential to change the way one thinks about fundraising.

It is my wish that someday someone will pick up where I left off and improve and expand on each topic about in this text. I hope that this book may be a valuable resource for new and experienced fundraisers alike in expanding their relational knowledge as they continue to serve others.

Please note that all literature reviews are documented in the text, as well as in the bibliography at the end of the book. All statistical findings are listed on page 181, under appendix A, and the survey sample can be found under appendix B on page 201.

Acknowledgements

I would like to extend my gratitude to a number of people who assisted in making the production of this book possible. First thanks to my wife, Barbara, for her counsel and support while working on this writing project. I also wish to extend gratitude to all sixteen survey participants for their input in this book's production. Their encouragement and the comments they provided greatly enhanced the quality of this book.

Many thanks to all my readers for their helpful feedback, especially to my dear friend Ronald D. Blaum, who reviewed the manuscript from an experienced fundraiser's perspective. His reassurance, critique, and creative appraisal was extremely helpful. His guidance and wisdom was priceless which comes as a result of his many years of experience in the field of philanthropy, especially with regards to charitable legacy planning.

I want to thank a number of college and university presidents who provided me with the opportunity to discover and develop my beginner skills in fundraising. I am grateful to the Mennonite Central Committee Great Lakes staff, especially those with whom I worked most closely.

I am indebted to my dear, longtime friend Mr. Solomon Belete, who wrote the forward for this book, for his counsel, encouragement, and valuable feedback throughout the process of writing this book. As a director of philanthropy, his ideas, expertise, and suggestions helped raise the quality of this book.

Finally, I thank Carter McKay-Epp for his help in editing this book. He was helpful in the early process of shaping the manuscript and offered countless counsel through arranging this book for publication.

Foreword

I had the distinct pleasure of reviewing the book *Funding A Mission, One Donor and One Penny at a Time* by Zenebe Abebe, Ph.D. I have known Dr. Abebe for nearly fifty years, having attended high school together at The Bible Academy in Nazareth, Ethiopia. My overall impression of my friend and colleague has been extremely positive, as he is someone that has dedicated his entire private and professional life to service and mission. He epitomizes the true meaning of mission, which is what this book is all about. He thoughtfully and meticulously shows the connection between mission and fundraising.

This book is an excellent contribution to our understanding and appreciation of philanthropy. The book is divided into four sections: I. Looking Ahead and Setting the Parameter; II. Planning and Strategizing; III. Framework for Action; IV. Sharing Ideas and Words of Encouragement.

In the introduction, Zenebe sets the context for why he pursued writing this manuscript. Unlike many writings on the topic, this has a personal imprint that one feels reverberating throughout the entire book. You cannot separate the author from the subject matter that he covers so thoroughly and with great passion and conviction. He himself did not approach fundraising as just a technical task to be accomplished. Rather, fundraising is a deeply felt aspiration and motivation to achieve greater meaning by alleviating pain and creating opportunities for those disenfranchised in our world. Funding a Mission reads like a personal manifesto.

In many respects, the book is a reflection of the author's strong commitment to just causes, depicting how he has applied both the art and science of fundraising in academia, international relief work, and many other global humanitarian projects. While many of us can separate our life from our work, Zenebe has been able to weave the two together, which is why his experience, albeit unique, has been fulfilling and transformative.

A common theme is the centrality of mission in fundraising. An equally important feature of the book is the light he shines on the role of donors and supporters. Mission and donors are juxta positioned with fundraisers as the brokers and the real glue that holds the relationship together. Zenebe has poured

Foreword

numerous examples and personal testimonials into the book to illustrate the important relationship he was able to forge with donors and the impact this has had on his service and leadership in particular, his almost six years as Executive Director at MCC Great lakes Region.

Let me digress for a moment to explain why I agree with him and the emphasis he has placed on Mission. In my view, mission is where the rubber meets the road, as it is in the mission statements of organizations that values and principles are embedded. The values of donors are found and expressed in mission statements and when they don't, there is a divide between the donor and the nonprofit. The important role of fundraisers is to find donors whose values unequivocally align with that of the organization to broker a mutually beneficial relationship. I refer to this as "symbiotic philanthropy."

Fundraisers are therefore important leaders in our nonprofit organizations. They are not always recognized and valued for their leadership role. The experiences Zenebe chronicles in the book clearly describe fundraisers as leaders who are in the business of "mission advancement." Thankfully, he has elevated their status to one of great importance in philanthropy. I am certain that he sees fundraising and fundraisers broadly

Funding A Mission

consisting of individuals who are involved as ambassadors, advocates, and askers—the triple A, to borrow from Kay Sprinkel Grace. Zenebe pays particular attention to a "culture of philanthropy," one in which staff, boards of directors, volunteers, and other stakeholders are involved in supporting and sustaining the organization. Fundraising is not a task that is compartmentalized to an individual or position. In a culture of philanthropy, the entire organization is involved in raising and promoting the organization and stewarding the donors and volunteers who are the financial backbone. Zenebe is clearly a strong proponent of this type of fundraising in order to be successful with any organization's mission and purpose.

Another undercurrent in the book is the fact that we live in a world that exemplifies both the best and the worst of humankind. Here in the United States, we have been able to show how human talent and ingenuity can be deployed to significantly improve our standard of living. We are a technological giant and are at the cutting edge of applying our intellectual capital to modernize all our spheres of life. At the same time, we are witnessing tremendous gaps in wealth and other sorts of disparity. It is this gap that nonprofits are called to address and mitigate in order to engender a spirit of hope and opportunity for all. Philanthropy is the space within, in which one remains optimistic and forward looking.

Donors, small and large, and volunteers who care deeply about mission are an essential means by which philanthropy can overcome some of the unrelenting challenges we face. This situation was what has motivated Zenebe to dedicate his personal and professional life to this important ministry of social justice. He has placed his trust in what ordinary people and passionate donors can do to change the trajectory of the future.

Zenebe prescribes a "donor-centric" approach to fundraising, which is what he attributes the success of his work to while at MCC Great Lakes. A donor-centric framework requires fundraisers to invest time and resources in donor cultivation, communication, and stewardship. He reinforces the importance of storytelling and full transparency as a strategy to build sustainable financial support. Communication through various channels builds confidence and demonstrates the impact that donors have on your organization. Strategic Planning is a mere exercise in futility without the ability to track and measure impact. Fundraisers are an integral part of the strategic planning process. These topics are introduced and covered with some depth in Section II of the book.

The role of the board has also been mentioned on a number of occasions. Zenebe underscores the critical contributions they make in terms of giving and sharing their own wealth and treasure. Board members are also pivotal in facilitating contact and the acquisition of new donors. Zenebe also notes how first-time donors are priceless, and I share his strong sentiments. Donors need to be asked to give, and once they do so, it is imperative that we do all that we can to thank them and hold on to them for the long-run. Our national statistics on donor retention are quite abysmal, and more attention is needed in order to maximize the return on investment. The donor lifecycle is an area that has tremendous importance.

Zenebe did not go through a formal training program in fundraising, as is the case with hundreds and thousands of fundraisers. He therefore promotes the need for both formal and informal training, mentorship and coaching, and affiliation with networks that are focused on philanthropy. One can become more skilled in areas like endowments, bequests, and planned gifts by participating in online programs or in training that is provided by the Association of Fundraising

Professionals (AFP) as well as the Sanford Institute of Philanthropy affiliates.

Donors expect organizations to have the skills to engage them in the proper way. An organization that has the skills and capacity to understand and engage donors' philanthropic drives is likely to benefit financially and scale its work. Donors also expect organizations to be transparent and accountable. This is even more relevant with regards to millennial donors. The book definitely touches on these essential fundraising topics, and there is more extensive writing on them as transparency, accountability, diversity, equity, and inclusion have taken the front stage.

Another interesting point that Zenebe makes is the need to empower the recipients of nonprofit organizations in order to build greater independence and self-sufficiency. The recipients are not just those who receive services but also those who are supporters and stakeholders of the organization in more ways than securing its financial health. Donors want to see their dollars stretch and are eager to see the changes and transformation of those who are on the receiving end. They want to see that there is a light at the end of the tunnel. Nonprofits inadvertently create a dependency relationship with their clients, especially those providing direct services, by not empowering them to assume a greater role and responsibility in sharing their destiny.

Finally, the book ends with great words of advice and wisdom. I encourage readers to read this section for more inspiration, especially those who are actively involved in fundraising. Dr. Abebe has written this book to share his experiences but also to challenge the reader and indulge them in some of the ideas he puts forward.

Missions, and the fundraising that is required to support them, are noble, extraordinary opportunities. Fundraising is an act that is honorable since its ultimate goal is to support causes for the common good.

I conclude by stating that there aren't many books where an author uses his own personal and professional experience as a case study to identify key ideas and principles. This book does exactly that with such clarity and candor. You will have a more positive outlook of fundraising and a greater appreciation of donors. You will feel more positive and confident in the future of philanthropy. I guarantee it!

Solomon Belette, Director, Sanford Institute of Philanthropy John F. Kennedy University Education for Change Pleasant Hill, CA

Introduction

More than anything, I'm writing this book out of a desire to share the stories of my fundraising experience as executive director of Mennonite Central Committee's (MCC) Great Lakes Office. I will detail how I was impacted and inspired by the trust and compassion of the generous people who supported our organization.

Secondly, I will share how my work with nonprofits has opened my eyes to the world's endless conflict: the never-ending crises that have brought all kinds of nonprofits together to help those in need.

I have come to realize that this is an ever-changing world, in which we are increasingly confronted with economic disparity, corruption, and unethical leaders. As a result of the corruptness of our world, we have allowed ourselves to become numb and accepting of the global rise of authoritarianism. We sit passively as the effects of climate change continue to be major threat to the future of humankind.

Over the years, we have witnessed, in all corners of the world, massive migrations that have resulted in unspeakable conditions for countless refugees. We have time and again seen the separation of family members, even young children from their parents.

In today's political ethos, telling the truth has become taboo, and politicians continue their vicious lies even when they are confronted with facts. In today's world, a select few power and money hungry people are responsible for the grief imposed on millions of people.

Thirdly, we cannot overstate how much the unchecked violence present in our world is a concern to many nonprofit fundraisers and their compassionate and peace-loving donors.

I have seen lives changed by the work of nonprofits around the world. Indeed, I have heard stories and witnessed occurrences where the support of nonprofit organizations coupled with adequate financial resources helped communities stand on their own after a crisis.

In what appears to be a world of chaos and confusion, philanthropy staff remain hopeful that working with donors who share their visions will inevitably lead to a better future for all uprooted and displaced peoples.

It is true that we can offer no simple explanation for their situation, nor can we

Introduction

guarantee its betterment. The hope that fundraisers and donors provide is a voice of compassion and an understanding that we will work tirelessly to support them.

In our constantly changing world, riddled with misunderstanding, only truth and honesty bring donors and nonprofit fundraisers together to offer hope to the needy. Our goal is to empower the next generation to be compassionate and remain driven by a love for others.

In 2010, when I accepted the position as executive director (CEO) at MCC Great Lakes region, I started looking inwards to affirm myself that I was a good leader and an experienced manager. I knew that I could be trusted and that I would be dedicated to the mission of the institution.

On the other hand, I was also naive and overconfident because I had not yet been tested in the field of nonprofit fundraising. Fortunately, my experience educated me thoroughly.

Since beginning my journey as a nonprofit fundraiser, I gained an understanding of the work of nonprofit organizations. I came to understand the value of building relationships as being fundamental to the profession that is philanthropy.

I now understand that building relationships between fundraisers and donors creates trust. It is trust that enables donors to give, simply because donors believe we will do what we say we will do with the support they provide.

I learned to view professional fundraising as a source of fulfillment, accomplishment, and personal growth. I am profoundly grateful for the opportunity I had to lead, serve, and learn at MCC. Throughout the book, I will share profound moments from my nonprofit fundraising journey. As a Kenyan would say, "Traveling is learning."

Section 1

Looking Ahead and Setting the Parameters

- Commitment to a Mission
- Guiding Principles
- Being Devoted to Your Mission
- Historical Context
- On-the-job Training
- How Much Wealth is There, and Who Needs It the Most
- Preparedness
- Looking for Generous Individuals
- Sharing the Wealth
- Finding Partners in Fundraising

Commitment to a Mission

Since the title of this book is Funding a Mission, it is imperative that I explain what mission means in the context of this book. I want to be sure we have an agreed upon definition of mission to avoid confusion.

It would be unusual to find any nonprofit organization, big or small, without a mission or purpose statement. *In the Chronicle of Philanthropy*, Alan Cantor who is a consultant for fundraising for people in government chronicle of higher education says (June 2018) "A mission statement is a building block of charitable fundraising." (p.40)

"Our good deeds should be motivated by a sincere desire to help others. Public recognitions should not be the goal."

Unknown Author

"Mission" has many meanings, and the word is used to say different things to different people. Upon seeing the word mission, people may think of missionary work or a church with only one purpose, that being to save souls. Others see mission as a region dependent on a larger church or denomination.

Dan Ebener, in his book *Leadership Wisdom from the Beatitudes* (1989), asserts that, "mission is like an anchor that keeps the organization grounded." (p.76) Others in the nonprofit field see a well-written mission statement as something that connects employees and their values to the organization and its task. Interestingly, according to Dictionary.com, the origins of the word mission lead back to 1590-1600 where it was used to mean "sending off." For the purpose of this book, we will give the word Mission a working definition to mean Purpose.

In his marvelous book *The Mission Myth: Building Nonprofit Momentum Through Business*, Moloney (2012) demonstrates the importance of having a mission: "Your mission matters. It's the whole reason you work at your organization. It's why you go through the challenges, face the crises, as for the money, and maneuver so many stakeholder relationships each and every day." (p. 288)

Others in the field warn that a nonprofit organization must have a meaningful mission statement, but achieving it is a lot harder than it sounds.

A mission can be thought of as a self-imposed objective or purpose, set to bring about changes. For example, it could take the form of a specific task that a person or group is charged to fulfill in helping victims of a natural disaster.

Throughout our history, and even today, faith-based organizations have been tied to charity work. In other words, it has always been the mission of faith-based organizations to help others. For centuries, service has been a driving force for charitable giving.

Most of us working in relief and development function in a crisis mode. But in his book *A Spirituality of Fundraising*, author Henri Nouwen (2010), has other ideas. "From the perspective of the gospel, fundraising is not a response to a crisis, Fundraising is, first and foremost, a form of ministry." (p.16) Nouwen, who calls fundraising itself a mission, also addresses the issues of giving and receiving and the relationship we have with money from the Biblical perspective. He documents the following Bible verses to serve as examples for how the Bible says we should address this relationship: (Prov.29:18), (2nd

Kings 21:1-90), (Acts 18:9), (Ps.1:3). (Isa.43:19), Luke 15:14-20), (Matt.16:23), (Rom. 12:2), (2nd Cor.9:11), (Eph.3:20), and (1st Cor.13:8, 1st Cor.14:1) (p.16-18).

The word "give" is significant in the Bible. In the King James Version of the Bible, give is mentioned 880 times. As we all understand, helping those in need is one of the major themes of the Bible and of Jesus's ministry. Both the Old and New Testament writings provide many examples of the importance of service and charity. One advocate of fundraising was the Apostle Paul who praised the Macedonians for giving to the church, even when they were poor themselves.

Giving to the needy is expected and very much Biblical, as Illustrated in 2nd Corinthians 9:7. It reads: "each of you should give what you have decided in your heart to give, not reluctantly or under compulsion, for God loves a cheerful giver."

As a donor once told me, when he and his wife give, they do so with joy. They know the gift is no longer theirs and they have no control over it. He further said that if they believe in the mission of the organization to whom they give funds, they trust the staff to manage it and that it is their responsibility. I have no doubt that, because of the generosity and, indeed, the mission of such givers, our world can and will become a better place. Thus, one can see the power of mission. It is mission that drives charitable organizations to help the needy across the globe. It is mission that spurs fundraisers to seek out those who identify with that mission and therefore offer their generous support.

It is mission that inspires compassionate giving by donors. As Peter Brinckerhoff states in his book *Smart Stewardship for Nonprofits (2012):* "Your mission is worth more than your buildings, more than your bank account and, yes, worth more than your volunteers, board, or staff. Why? Because the mission is why those people show up." (p. 20)

The power of mission lies in its ability to unify and inspire. The roles of all involved in an organization may be different, but their mission, their purpose, is what brings them together.

No matter how good your mission statement is, it is imperative that your mission statement not be written in stone. An organization must realize the inevitability of change. For example, your program or organization may grow or shrink in scale to adjust to various circumstances. Depending on the kind of shift your organization experiences, its mission statement may need to be adjusted accordingly.

Mission statements need to be revisited and sometimes revised because of changes faced by organizations. For nonprofit organizations, is it critical to look at what needs to be changed to maintain the health of the organization.

The city where I live is reorganizing the school system and closing high schools—some as old as 132 years old—because of low enrollment. Many private colleges are shrinking or closing for a variety of reasons. Church conferences are losing member congregations because of cultural or biblical interpretation disputes. These examples showcase situations in which revisiting a mission statement could be helpful.

Rewriting or at least revisiting a mission statement is a step that should be taken in the advent of such divisions seen within those groups. A well-articulated mission is your organization's source of collective power that propels it toward its goals.

Comments from survey respondents (Research Question 4)

Our mission statement is key to connecting to our constituents and donors. We have a specific marketing piece that allows us to clearly communicate our mission statement and create interest from donors and potential donors.

Historically, we have had 100% participation from our board of directors and >90% participation from employees. Alumni participation averages 28% which is above average among our peer schools.

We have sought to cultivate a culture of philanthropy among employees so that they are aware of advancement opportunities when they are engaging in other ways with our constituents.

There are times when I am challenged to relate to people who do not hold the exact same personal values that I do, but my job is to connect the donor to the organization, not to build the relationship only with me.

When survey participants were asked if their organization had a written mission statement with objectives to provide guidance in fundraising, 30% of the respondents reported that they did not have a mission statement.

This was a big surprise to the researcher, who expected all organizations to have some kind mission statement.

69% of participants admitted to having a statement with written objectives

30% said they do not have one

Guiding Principles

Whereas a mission statement is a broad description of an organization's overall purpose, the guiding principles of an organization give additional insight into its direction.

Similar to an organization's mission, its guiding principles are a series of clarifying statements. These statements may then serve as a guide for all organization's board members and staff, as well as its donors.

Reading through the guiding principles of a nonprofit organization should help to clarify the purpose of said organization as they will provide more details.

> "No man will make a great leader who wants to do it all himself, or to get all the credit for doing it."
>
> **Andrew Carnegie**

Funding A Mission

Every nonprofit should develop a basic understanding of what they want to do and why. It is the guiding principles that provide a greater degree of specificity as to how the mission will be carried out. By following the guiding principles, there should be a consistency in execution and greater assurance that things are being done right. Your organization's guiding principles further explain what your organization does and why. Furthermore, your organization's principles will let employees know what to expect and how the organization will operate.

For organizations that do not already have a series of guiding principles, the following eight-point framework is offered as a guide for your future fundraising efforts:

1. You join others who come to aid the oppressed because you believe that someday the oppressed will rise to stand on their own.
2. You are aware of the limited resources around us and believe in good stewardship and the effective management of your resources.
3. You will do your best to maintain the trust of those who support the organization.

4. You believe in raising funds for projects, and you will always be prepared to tell the stories of your outcomes.
5. You have budget and spending plans, and you are accountable to inform donors and stakeholders of results in a timely manner.
6. To you, seeking donations from your supporters is a calling, and you take it seriously.
7. Because donors reach out to support what you do out of their own free will, generosity, and grace, you are to extend that same grace to the needy with respect and dignity.
8. Advancing your mission may be one of your end goals; however, assisting people to move from where they are to where they want to be must be your principal objective.

When we sense that we are called to do something, we see it as something greater than work. We see it as something done with compassion to make a lasting positive impact on the lives of others. President Barack Obama once said, "if you go out and make some good things happen, you will fill the world with hope, you will fill yourself with hope."

Being Devoted to Your Mission

Being involved in writing an organization's mission statement is quite different from being devoted to that mission. Before new team members are hired to work for an organization, they must demonstrate their own devotion to its mission. They must acknowledge that the organization's written mission statement aligns with their own interests and goals, as they must have credibility when meeting with donors. When an organization's staff is prepared to passionately serve the organization, that organization is ready to fulfill its mission.

"My mission in life is not merely to survive, but to thrive; and to do so with some passion, some humor, and some style."

Maya Angelou

An organization's mission statement is a living testimony to the passion of its members. However, it is always paramount that an organization's mission statement be revised if it is found to no longer serve the organization.

It helps an organization's fundraisers if the organization's fundraising philosophy is based on a sound mission statement. This helps fundraisers focus on specific goals that are relevant to the organization's mission. An organization's mission is not the same as its objectives, for they are derived from its mission statement.

An organization's mission statement is what makes it stand out in the public eye. It defines the organization. Moreover, an organization's commitment to its mission must be affirmed by how it communicates, both in its publications and its public image.

For an organization to progress from where it is to where its members want it to be, its members must follow the organization's mission statement as their guide. An organization's mission statement is an excellent way for the organization to articulate its distinctive purpose to donors and to develop a culture of philanthropy.

For example, it is a good idea to present potential donors with your organization's mission statement before asking for donations.

Your organization's mission, after all, should represent the core of what your organization does. Naturally, it is more effective to ask for donations once potential donors have already bought into your organization's mission.

Many scholars have written on mission and commitment. Peter Brinckerhoff, an expert on nonprofit management, has taken strong interest in writing about mission. Brinckerhoff (2012), in his book *Smart Stewardship for Nonprofits: Making the Right Decision in Good Times and Bad*, defines mission as an organization's most valuable asset. (p.52) He argues that mission is why an organization's board and staff show up to their jobs. No organization can exist without a mission.

Steven Rothschild (2012), suggests that the success of any organization depends on using its mission to guide its actions. In the words of Rothschild, a clearly defined mission operationalizes an organization's purpose.

Your organization can easily be identified by its mission statement. If donors like your organization's mission, they will support your organization, and if they do not agree with its mission, they may not support your organization. Thus, your organization's mission helps you build relationships with potential donors.

Comments from survey respondents
(Research question 24)

Fundraising is ministry. It takes drive and courage to do the work, but it takes a pastoral care and sensitivity to do it well with donors. I recommend the little book The Spirituality of Fundraising by Henri Nouwen as a resource. I require my staff to read through it every year.

Our mission statement is key to connecting to our constituents and donors. We have a specific marketing piece that allows us to clearly communicate our mission statement and create interest from donors and potential donors.

Historically, we have had 100% participation from our board of directors and >90% participation from employees. Alumni participation averages 28% which is above average among our peer schools.

We have sought to cultivate a culture of philanthropy among employees so that they are aware of advancement opportunities when they are engaging in other ways with our constituents.

Historical Context

What we do today as trained fundraisers may be done less effectively by untrained fundraisers. Yet, even the most effective fundraisers have to start somewhere. Everything has its beginning.

The art of fundraising has a long history, one that has been constantly honed over many years. There was a time when money was raised locally, with much less fanfare, and no strategic plans. Fundraisers often would have gone door-to-door asking for donations. For the most part, nonprofit organizations used volunteers to help them raise funds in the early years of the profession.

> "A people without the knowledge of their past history, origin, and culture is like a tree without roots."
>
> **Marcus Garvey**

Here are some historical perspectives regarding fundraising: It has been documented that early fundraising in the United States began with the Young Men's Christian Association (YMCA) and Harvard University in the early 1900s. Further review of the literature shows that the National Society of Fund Raisers (NSFR) started with more organized professional fundraising trainings around the country in the 1960s.

Today, nonprofit organizations, small and large, base their fundraising work on extensive research about their potential donors. It is very common for an organization to have a fully-paid director leading its fundraising efforts. These directors develop strategic plans for targeting donors, create benchmarks to measure success, and set in place timelines that help them to measure and compare outcomes.

In addition to fundraising, titles such as "resource generation," "development," "constituency relation," and "advancement" are all used to define what we do today to raise money to support nonprofit organizations around the globe.

As for this book, let's call it what it is: fundraising. I remember a conversation I had with one of my staff I'll call Robert. When we switched from donor relations to fundraising, Robert, a part-time employee, ordained

Historical Context

minister, and member of the fundraising team, was not a fan of the name change. He was adamant about not using the word fundraising. Robert explained to me that he would be ashamed to stand in front of constituencies to ask them to give money to his organization.

When I asked him why, Robert explained to me that donors already knew what our organization does, so they didn't always need a reminder to give us money.

I reminded Robert that, as a pastor, he stands in front of his congregation every Sunday asking church members to give their money to his church. I said to him, "If that isn't considered fundraising for the mission of the church, what is?" I explained to Robert that the idea of asking for money or other resources was very Biblical. I have my suspicions that my colleague Robert may have not read Henri Nouwen (2010), who said in *A Spirituality of Fundraising*, "Asking people for money is giving them the opportunity to put their resources at the disposal of the Kingdom." (p. 45)

My conversation with Robert reminded me of Millard Fuller's observation about asking for money, and as he put it, "I have tried raising money by asking for it, and by not asking for it. I always got more by asking for it."

If Robert and other staff were not attuned to the fundraising portion of their organization, they may have felt that bringing money into the organization was someone else's job or that the process of fundraising was not inherent to the organization's success.

What Robert did not understand is the fact that an organization's donors want to hear that we need their support. In fact, according to Nicole Wallace, "[recently] giving declined across every age group and every income and education level." Perhaps a partial explanation for this across-the-board decline in giving is the fact that organizations need to be clearer about articulating their needs.

As executive director at MCC Great Lakes, it was my responsibility to communicate to all my staff what we were going to do as a team. As it happened, my expectations and management style may have been radically different from my teams'. I explained to the staff that having a reluctance to ask for donations was an unacceptable attitude in our fundraising plan going forward. We couldn't meet our fundraising goals by expecting things to happen without making an effort to tell our story.

Donors want to be asked to give. As the saying goes, "ask and it shall be given to you". Asking is important. If you need help, ask for help. Fundraisers must know the financial requirements for carrying out an organization's mission and making a real difference in people's lives. Soon after I took office at MCC Great Lakes, I invited author and consultant, Rebekah Basinger, to spend a day with my fundraising team in 2011. She strongly recommended not be afraid to ask money for our mission. She reminded us of a reality present at nonprofits: *"no money no mission,"* she said.

Henri Nouwen encourages us to not see fundraising as a burden, but rather to see the work of fundraising as a joyful and hope-filled expression of ministry.

Of course, the Bible also provides plenty of examples of fundraising. An example that quickly comes to mind is Matt. 7:7, which reads, "Ask and it will be given to you; seek and you will find; knock and the door will be open to you." These are active verbs. The message is that there is work to be done in fundraising.

If you are in charge of a fundraising team, it is good to use language that is clear to you, your staff, and your organization's donors. Be sure that there is no confusion about what you are saying. Ultimately, fundraising starts with a relationship. If you don't know the donor or have difficulties communicating with them, it is hard and uncomfortable to ask for money. While I worked at MCC Great Lakes, our fundraising strategy was built on relationships with current and potential donors.

I and others at my organization learned from our personal experiences that fundraising is simply what a person does to collect money from people they know, or sometimes from people they don't know, by explaining the mission of the institution for which they are raising funds.

It is an important effort to consistently build and maintain current relationships with donors while also reaching out to form new ones. Whether done by letters, emails, or face-to-face, it is critical that you, the fundraiser, present the uniqueness of your organization's mission using clear and simple language.

It is also critical that you fundraise with confidence, hopefulness, and excitement. With strong fundraiser-donor relationships comes the opportunity to tell them more about an organization's history.

Explain each portion of your organization's mission with detail and clarity. For example, if one of your organization's goals is to provide clean drinking water to those who need it, explain as much as you can about who is in need of water, the location and costs of your projects, and your organization's success stories.

Another important aspect of fundraising is the leadership within each fundraising division. A lead fundraiser or director must always inform the entire staff about all aspects of current funding issues, educating them in the current methodology.

As fundraisers, we collect funds to help our organizations meet their goals, and we also act as leaders who help our organizations move forward.

Fundraisers must have diverse qualities of leadership, such as being empowering, negotiating, compromising and informing to be able to serve their supporters. We lead as we communicate and relate to donors, staff, and board members. As we grow and try to be better stewards, we must learn new ways of doing things. Doing things the way we've always done them is not a sign of good leadership. Conversely, learning new ways to do things makes us better leaders.

Good leaders are those rooted in their guiding principles and their organization's mission statement. Good leaders find new ways to learn and then teach their strategies to others.

It is a sign of a good leader, if a fundraiser is able to effectively inform donors about wealth management and planned giving. A good leader will consistently inform donors about new products, such as changes in tax laws and options in the market, as well as opportunities for continuing their education with optional workshops and seminars for supporters.

A good fundraiser will present their organization's needs and then invite their donors to contribute to a specific project they feel passionate about. The more a donor feels personally connected to a project the more they will be willing to help it achieve its goal. Being a fundraiser is to be a leader in all aspects of your organization and its constituency.

Being fully engaged and staying current in all matters of your organization is a sign of a good quality.

On-the-job Training

On-the-job training is encouraged by most businesses and educational institutions. Some call it practical training. Others call it an internship. Regardless of its labels, it is extremely well endorsed. Prospective employees are very much favored if they have been involved in on-the-job training.

On-the-job training may be the best way to learn the tools of the fundraising trade. In the words of the accomplished psychologist, Albert Bandura, people learn best by observing the people around them. Thus, new fundraisers will gain key skills simply through observing their colleagues.

"Tell me and I forget. Teach me and I remember. Involve me and I learn."

Benjamin Franklin

As for the merits of on-the-job training, there are many books, trainings, and scholarly articles written on the subject. I also recommend that you visit philanthropy.edu/thefundraisingschool for a more detailed course of study.

I can personally attest to the merits of on-the-job training, as I gained many of my fundraising and management skills during my own on-the-job training. I can say that my fundraising experience has been cultivated in two lines of work, one of those areas being college and university-related work and the other being relief and development work. Through working in both of these areas, I was able to sharpen my skills and learn more about the importance and influence of compassion, integrity, and commitment in the nonprofit fundraising world.

When I was hired as the executive director for MCC Great Lakes, I was expected to be the face of the organization. This meant that I had to be involved in fundraising in a significant way. After all, fundraising should be a part of every executive director's job description.

I quickly observed that there were, and continue to be, four main income streams for MCC: thrift shops, individual giving, relief sales, and congregational giving. These four income streams are well-developed to support the fundraising activities in Mennonite communities, both in the United States and in Canada. Having these four solid income streams has helped anchor MCC's mission and philosophy.

The long-standing nature of these income streams made fundraising a lot easier for me as the new executive director. Early on in my training for the position, I was able to recognize and appreciate the fact that there were already a good number of reasonably happy donors and volunteers within the organization.

Prior to arriving at MCC Great Lakes, I spent over 35 years working at four faith-based colleges and universities. During my years at these nonprofit schools, I served as a dean of student life, Vice President for Multicultural Education, Vice President for Equity and Inclusion, and an associate professor of psychology.

When I worked in academia, my job description never included fundraising as a primary responsibility. However, fundraising by way of grant writing was an expected role of each position. At these institutions, it was normal for a group of those working for support services programs to come together to write grants to support the operations of our offices with soft money—grants and other gifts outside the annual budget of the university.

Funding A Mission

From my previous work experience in academia, which was on-the-job training that would eventually aid me heavily in my job as executive director of MCC Great Lakes.

Today, at nonprofit higher education institutions, student services programs, such as multicultural education and other enrichment programs, are not top economic priorities. As a result, the pressure on the staff of these organization's to either raise money to keep the programs going or to discontinue them was always present when considering annual budget issues.

At these institutions, I learned about the importance of budgeting, management, accountability, and trust in fundraising for the continued survival of a program. Learning about the importance of fundraising in academia helped me to understand its significance when I joined MCC Great Lakes.

From the moment I was introduced to MCC's programs, its mission, and its goals, I was impressed by the organization before I began working at MCC, it had been a well-run, well-known, and well-managed institution, not only nationally but also worldwide. What I had heard about MCC was quickly confirmed by what I saw once I joined the organization.

The loyalty of the staff and board at MCC Great Lakes and their relationships with their

On-the-job Training

supporters was easily noticeable. I also noted how MCC Great Lakes' community trusted it, respected it, and consequently funded its mission.

Early on as a fundraiser, I learned that fundraising was not simply a command or a demand for people to give but the ability to relate to others and to invite giving.

Fundraising is not done from a position of authority or control but from a point of love and concern for others.

If you are working at a well-established organization like MCC, where a donor database is in place and continually updated, fundraising will be much more enjoyable.

When I started working for MCC Great Lakes, it was clearly written in my job description that I should spend 30% of my time fundraising. The following year, it was increased to 50%. Soon after that, the board of directors asked me to work full-time as a fundraiser. Beginning in my first year as CEO, my staff and I at MCC Great Lakes were given a goal to raise 5 million to 8 million dollars every year. Luckily, MCC's global reputation made it easier for my staff and I to meet that goal every year for five and a half years and until my retirement.

My present understanding of fundraising at nonprofit organizations can be attributed to the confidence I developed from my time in academia, from my five and half years of fundraising at MCC, and from my keen interest in listening to experts in the field at a number of seminars and workshops I attended throughout my career.

I enjoy and am confident in fundraising today because I learned through doing. As a result of my positive experiences, I would often encourage college students to pursue internships at MCC. It was my hope, that if they experienced how a nonprofit works while at MCC, they would someday become leaders at impactful nonprofits.

I believed then, as I still do today, that hands-on experiences are critical for career development. My fundraising skills were developed not only from reading or from classroom lectures, but also from working in the field and from observing my peers. The drive to be involved and to always willing to learn, drove me to seek out true fundraising experiences. I was always ready to learn and would not have been successful in my career without learning from others at MCC and elsewhere.

Comments from survey respondents (Research question 2)

I began learning about fundraising while serving on boards and when I accepted my current development job, I began a more formal training program.

I can't tell you how much I appreciate what you are attempting to do by documenting your experience in fundraising.

It is time for us to do what we do well by listening and learning sometimes from one another. This is one way to keep learning. I have been in sessions with some high powered and highly paid consultant who simply told us what we already know. I hope you can tell some of your fundraising stories.

How Much Wealth Is There, and Who Needs It the Most?

Discerning the amount of wealth in the world at any given time is almost an impossible task. The answer is a moving target. The amount always changes, as it often depends on the current condition of the wealthiest nations. According to the Credit Suisse *Global Wealth Report 2018* during the 12-month to mid-2018, aggregate global wealth rose by $14.0 trillion (4.6%) to the combined total of $317 trillion outpacing population growth.

> "Rich people should consider that they are only trustees for what they possess and should show their wealth to be more in doing good than merely in having it."
>
> **Joseph Hall**

Some estimates predict that there could be anywhere from $36.8 trillion to $90.4 trillion dollars in the world. The question for nonprofit organizations is, "Who needs the money, and how much will we need to raise to help those people in need?" This is a simple question without a simple answer.

Bill Gates, co-chairman of the Bill & Melinda Gates Foundation, argues that it is not fair that we have so much wealth when billions of others have so little. Bill Gates and Melinda Gates, who are globally-recognized philanthropists, are known for having given away billions of dollars, because they understand the global issue of unfair wealth distribution.

Many in the field of wealth management, including Melanie Curtin, a writer and activist, argue that only eight men control the vast majority of the world's wealth. Curtin states that six of the eight men are Americans from the American tech community. For most fundraisers, it would be unfathomable that you would ever meet one of these people.

George William Domhoff (2018), of the University of California at Santa Cruz writes that in the United States, wealth is highly concentrated in relatively few hands. As of 2013, the top 1% of households—the upper class—owned 36.7% of all privately held wealth, and ... only 11% of wealth for the bottom 80% wage and salary workers.

A more detailed, statistical explanation of wealth distribution in America can be found in Domhoff's book (2014) *Who Rules America? The Triumph of the Corporate Rich.*

An organization's donors may range from across the economic spectrum, from wealthy donors to low-income donors. Often an organization's supporters are middle-class individuals and families. Fundraisers should keep a donor's economic status in mind, being mindful to not ask for too much or too little. In the end, all of an organization's donors practice philanthropy, giving their hard-earned money to those in the world who need it most.

Preparedness

Preparedness in fundraising means everything. It means knowing your organization's focus for the year, knowing how to interact with your organization's donors, and knowing how to budget for the future. The basic elements of nonprofit fundraising preparation consist of planning ahead, getting organized, and executing your plan within a given time frame.

That said, preparedness means different things to different roles within a nonprofit, and this is certainly true for fundraisers. For all professionals, however, to be effective means to be prepared to do your job.

"Find out how much God has given you and from it take what you need; the remainder is needed by others."

Saint Augustine

Funding A Mission

If you are being hired as a fundraiser, it will be your responsibility to be prepared for your new job. It is recommended for those who are considering going into fundraising to join a regional association of fundraising professionals. You might seek out a mentor and develop a network of professionals that you can contact if you need to ask a question. Actual on-the-job experiences, like those gained from working with regional fundraising associations, will serve to both make a fundraiser more attractive for hiring and eventually more effective at their jobs.

Preparedness for new fundraisers may mean attending workshops and trainings. For others, it may mean observing and working with their peers. Indeed, for many, being prepared simply means to be interested in and passionate about fundraising.

A fundraiser needs to be prepared to do their work. It is true that there is no one way to solicit money. However, every fundraiser, new or experienced, will need a set of skills common to all fundraisers.

Some of the skills fundraisers should have may be hard to develop. For some skills, you either have them or you don't. Each person has a different gift. Some have the gift of public speaking. Others have the gift of writing. Others are great problem solvers. Each person should be prepared to make the greatest use of their personal gifts. Moreover, preparedness on an individual level means to be aware of how one's gifts can be used to help one's organization. No one fundraising style will serve all fundraisers.

Oftentimes, what preparedness means for a fundraiser depends on the mission of their organization. A fundraiser's skills should align with the skills needed to carry out their organization's mission and to communicate with their organization's donors.

For the most part, due to the smaller size of many nonprofits, most staff are expected to support the efforts of fundraising in any way they can. In these situations, being prepared means being willing and ready to be involved, even if it is not your primary job. From receptionists to board members, preparedness means to express gratitude to the donors and hardworking volunteers who make what the organization does possible.

Be mindful and realize that the primary goal of fundraisers should be to help others achieve self-sufficiency. As you prepare yourself and volunteers to help raise funds, be reminded that what you do is not always easy, but necessary to ease the pain of those in need. Being prepared as a fundraiser will set the stage for your success and the success of your organization. Being prepared will help you make a difference.

Looking for Generous Individuals

The essence of fundraising is in finding contacts, effectively communicating with those contacts, and, most of all, building friendships. Fundraising must focus on the formation of genuine, long-lasting friendships based on a common understanding of your organization's mission.

Remember that, simply put, fundraising means to ask individuals, corporations, and foundations to support your mission. Yet, before you ask for money, you should be in a position to explain your organization's cause and mission to donors.

"Generosity is the most natural outward expression of an inner attitude of compassion."

Dalai Lama

You must be mindful of the complexity that comes with approaching donors. What some donors have in mind may not be in the best interest of your organization. Your case for support must be clear. This can save you and your donors from second-guessing about where their money is going. Be clear in your "ask," whether you are seeking funding for new projects, current projects, or general operating expenses.

Those who understand and support your organization's mission will be generous people whose support is offered to move you and your organization from hopelessness to the possibility of new beginnings. As our world's problems grow and become more complex, it is going to take all of us to build a united global effort to improve our world. It is critical to mobilize and empower our donors for the good of the world as we assist those who are looking to improve their lives.

As transformational fundraisers, we look for donors who see the good in all people. Utilizing contributions from generous people, we not only offer hope to the hopeless, but we commit to building a new culture for a sustainable global community of the future. We have the potential to create a hopeful world if we harness the energy and resources of like-minded people in our communities.

Our call to do this work must be rooted in the mobilization and empowerment of donors for the good of the world.

The opportunity to raise funds is enormous. There are countless foundations, businesses, and individuals who are willing to support a good mission. According to a presentation by an employee of the Lilly Family School of Philanthropy, as much as 136 trillion dollars will be circulating over the next 35 years. Certainly, there is enough money for both individuals and foundations to donate.

My experiences in fundraising involved working with others, attending workshops, and, at times, misjudging or getting lost in the day-to-day detail of the task. I spent much time speaking; traveling locally, nationally, and internationally; and learning from the experiences of other fundraisers, as well as from those with "boots on the ground" implementing program.

I witnessed accounts and heard stories about communities that had become self-sustaining as a result of the determination of nonprofits. I also observed that these success stories were only possible because of the power that impact donors have on nonprofit organizations. This impact is rooted in one thing: It is clear to me that the most fundamental quality in the relationship between a fundraiser and his or her donors is trust.

In my experience, donors trusted what they heard from us at MCC Great Lakes regarding what we were going to do and that what we were doing would make a difference in people's lives. I quickly learned that one way to build trust with donors is to tell them stories that showcase the effectiveness of an organization's programs. Donors love to hear your stories.

One must remember that interacting with donors is a two-way street. Naturally, when you talk to donors, you must be prepared to respond to questions and to receive advice. Thomas Wolf in his book *How to Connect with Donors and Double the Money You Raise (2011)* quoted Bob Demont saying that when he asked people for money, they gave him advice, and when he asked them for advice, they gave him money. This is so relevant when it comes to my experience. I believe that this is true, as I have been the recipient of money, advise, and, of course, wisdom. I am very grateful for generous people and their friendship.

It is important, as one of my staff members taught me, to always thank your organization's donors. When you first meet a potential donor, thank them for their time. As you tell the stories of your organization and ask a donor for support, thank them for their interest in your organization. Finally, as you end your time with a donor, thank them again, especially if they have given a gift. Gratitude, like trust, is pivotal to the fundraiser-donor relationship.

I have also observed that a critical function of fundraising is to determine when, how, and what information you will need to share with others. Our world today is continually changing, more so than ever before. Our modes of communication have become better and more diverse, and there are many communication methods available to us today. For example, fundraisers can now communicate with donors using the lightning-fast tools of email, social media, and instant messaging. Even so, it is important for fundraisers to remember the value and importance of phone calls, letters, and face to face communication.

As a fundraiser, you must remember that the opportunities are many and that donors are diverse. Nevertheless, no matter who your donors are or how you communicate with them, you must also remember that they want to know not only what it is that your organization does, but also why it does what it does. It is also important to inform donors of your organization's timeline.

As a fundraiser, you must remember that fundraising is a process. Sometimes, forming relationships with donors is hard. It is about building trust, and trust is sometimes hard to build. Trust matters more than anything. Lauren Loktev makes a compelling argument in her article, "You should Treat Fundraising Like dating." (2016) Just like in romantic relationships, trust is hard to build and is easily destroyed.

Similarly, Martin Teitel, a foundation executive, has been quoted talking about the dynamic of fundraising this way: "...fundraising is like what dating was in high school...hard work intertwined with great risk and continual rejection."

Remember that the fundraising process carries with it the great promise of accomplishing great things.

Sharing the Wealth

In the United States and Canada, many nonprofit organizations raise funds from the same donor base. There are also other international agencies who draw from the same fundraising sources to support programs in developing countries. Although many people report on resource availability around the globe, it is hard to discern the true availability of those resources or find out who controls them.

There are fundraisers, particularly for international development programs, who believe that there are plenty of resources in the United States and Western Europe.

"The greatest good you can do for others is not just to share your riches, but to reveal to him his own."

Benjamin Disraeli

Those fundraisers often feel that those resources must be shared with those who need them. These are people who are supporters of missions or programs in developing countries. They see it as a responsibility of developed countries to give back to those countries who are in need of money to build up their infrastructure and human capital in the forms of education, health, and development work, especially if they have a stable government.

What these fundraisers do is admirable, and their vision and mission are to be commended. They believe that there is an unfair distribution of wealth and that the world's wealth must be redistributed to make a difference in the lives of the needy.

The work of these fundraisers has made a big difference in the building of infrastructure for schools, water wells, health care facilities, and churches. The concern is that, unless they are also involved in culturally appropriate mentoring and the empowering of indigenous citizens toward self-reliance, their efforts may not be sustainable.

Unlimited resources do not exist anywhere in the world. In an article published by Nicole Wallace in *The Chronicle of Philanthropy (2018)*, Wallace states that the share of Americans who donate to charity is falling behind. She further states that the share of giving has dropped most among 51 to 60-year-olds, who are often bedrock donors.

It is critical for fundraising professionals in both developed and developing countries to have an open and honest conversation about how to mentor, empower, and understand the limitations associated with their profession. Fundraisers should make a strong effort to understand the challenges and responsibilities that both sides face regarding current and future resource availability. The goal of helping others should be to create long term self-sufficiency.

Partnerships with international fundraisers should be encouraged. Together as partners, we can effectively respond to unanticipated humanitarian crises. However, the significant challenge of long-term development work to support day-to-day program expenses must be the obligation of local fundraisers.

Another way to look at it would be for international fundraisers to rethink their non-crisis response. Fundraisers from international countries have their own millionaires and billionaires who control their country's wealth and who could be nurtured to become major donors. The opportunities are there. Missing is the vision and the will to start something new. In the words of author and fundraiser Marshall McNott, helping another by enabling that person to become self-sufficient through a gift, a loan, or by helping them to gain a skill or employment is considered to be very important to the culture of philanthropy.

Following the same argument, Marla Pierson Lester, in *The Common Place* publication (2018) articulated that, "around the world, MCC partners with local organizations, communities, and churches in projects that empower and equip people to work for change for themselves and their neighbors." (p.10-11) This model of self-sufficiency is considered to be one of the best strategies for any nonprofit organization interested in empowering those they serve.

Finding Partners in Fundraising

From the get-go, the work of nonprofit fundraisers is to inform everyone about what your organization wants to achieve with the funds you raise. It is important to communicate to your donors that their donations will support your organization's mission. This is known as creating a culture of philanthropy.

> "We are one, our cause is one, and we must help each other; if we are to succeed."
>
> **Frederick Douglass**

To create this culture, it is not unusual to form partnership arrangements between two or more organizations that have similar interests and goals. We can observe impactful partnerships in the fields of education, business, and local government. These partnerships can ultimately serve the public good in their communities.

Some nonprofit organizations have the funds but lack the staffing to implement the services they wish to provide. Conversely, other organizations may have the staff to carry out their mission, but lack funding. The collaboration of such two agencies can serve to fulfill the missions and goals of both organizations.

I witnessed this type of partnership between two nonprofit organizations first hand while on learning tours in Colombia and in Cambodia. In both countries, the pair of agencies were not only happy with their collaboration but also with their outcomes. Everyone benefited.

If you are a leader of your organization, you may be short-staffed or too busy to do everything. Consider reaching out to experienced retired persons and volunteers to help you raise funds. Volunteers normally represent your donor community and can help you communicate your organization's mission to donors. They will often utilize social networking effectively to expand the scope and depth of their connections to donors in a way that would be difficult for you or your staff.

The Association of Fundraising Professionals (AFP), in their *Participants Fundraising Training Manual* (2010), highlighted the value of having volunteers as partners in fundraising. The following is a summary of a few key points given in the manual:

- Volunteers have the desire to give back
- Volunteers have the desire to develop skills or expertise
- Volunteers have the desire to build personal and professional relationships
- Volunteers have the desire to make a difference
- Volunteers have belief in the mission of your organization

Additionally, AFP suggests that if you want to utilize the help of volunteers, you must be sure to set realistic goals, empower them to accomplish their goals by providing them with appropriate training and by recognizing their efforts. If you have volunteers help you, it is only fair for you to acknowledge their efforts by including them in decision making, and, of course, by making what they do rewarding and interesting. Individual and public appreciation of your volunteers is strongly recommended.

Of course, when considering local partnerships in fundraising for your organization, reaching out to volunteers is just one option. There are many opportunities for partnerships. For example, MCC Great Lakes once invited three local business to join us in matching funds for a special project with which they were familiar. They happily joined us in a partnership lasting over five years and helped us to raise a significant amount of money.

As the majority of nonprofit organizations are often underfunded and lack publicity, forming local partnerships with businesses, educational systems, and service organizations in the community creates a better awareness of your brand.

What worked for MCC Great Lakes over the years were the partnerships we developed with local furniture stores and technology-based businesses. They provided us with special discounts when we purchased supplies and needed support services.

By realizing that partnerships can involve more than just fundraising, the opportunities are truly limitless. Nonprofit organizations do need the help of others in their communities to help them to raise money. However, when you explore partnerships with other agencies and businesses, be sure that you have a solid expectation and outcome in mind.

Section 2

Planning and Strategizing, Staying in Touch, and Building Trust

- Strategic Planning,
- Qualities and Measures of Success in Fundraising
- Board Involvement in Fundraising
- Listening to Donors
- Why People Give
- Legacy Donors
- First-Time Donors

Strategic Planning

In this section, I highlight the importance of strategic planning, organizational assessment, measurement, and outcomes.

What is strategic planning? It is an organization's process for defining its future direction and making decisions regarding the use of its resources and measuring outcomes. A strategic plan is an organizational playbook to help its board and staff move in union toward achieving a common goal.

A strategic plan entails more than just economics. For example, effective communication and marketing plans should be parts of an

> "The essence of strategy is choosing what not to do."
>
> **Michael Porter**

organization's strategic plan. With a strategic plan, an organization will be able to refine its direction, assess its needs, and understand its organizational strengths and weaknesses.

Interestingly, a number of survey respondents mentioned that their organizations did not have a strategic plan in place. Nonetheless, many of these respondents claimed that they wished for their organizations to develop a strategic plan in the future.

In my many years spent working in higher education and at MCC, I had the privilege of participating in the development of six different strategic plans, all of which centered around the idea of assessment and measurement. Of the six strategic plans, I served as a lead point-person on three of them.

A strategic plan includes a series of activities that help an organization articulate and refine its goals. Throughout the strategic planning process, an organization's executive director should lead its board and staff members to clearly define the organization's direction and purpose.

The process of developing a strategic plan is an opportunity for everyone within an organization to come together to articulate a shared understanding of how to achieve the organization's objectives and goals going forward. All staff, fundraising or not, must be part of the strategic planning process. This is because it is critical for everyone in an organization to know which way the organization is heading. A strategic plan serves as a roadmap to help guide an organization.

The creation of a strategic plan starts with a strategic planning document. Any strategic planning document should be developed by everyone in an organization, whether they work at the front desk or on the board. It is important to never forget the significance of this process, because the involvement of everyone is critical to securing their "buy-in" to its implementation going forward. The following four steps are recommended guidelines that an organization's executive director should utilize when guiding the creation of a strategic plan:

First, invite all stakeholders, which includes all your board and staff members, to be part of the process.

Second, together the team will draft or update your organization's mission statement.

Third, your team will go through a process to determine your organization's strengths, weaknesses, opportunities, and threats through what is known as SWOT analysis.

Fourth, your team will decide on the three to five-year timeline for your organization's plan—five years being the most commonly implemented duration.

A critical aspect of the strategic planning process is that an organization's goals and objectives are, or are made to be, achievable and measurable.

An organization's plan should be developed with a monitoring system in place. This can be done by designating a person or team who will be accountable for monitoring organizational activities each year (See Chart C) This person or team should also be accountable for providing a progress report that identifies specific benchmarks and their target dates for completion as agreed upon in the strategic planning process.

In particular, an organization must have criteria in place to assess each of its goals and objectives, at least annually. This annual assessment enables an organization to measure whether or not it achieved its intended goals. If an organization did not achieve its strategic goals, the annual assessment provides an opportunity to evaluate the cause or causes and the chance to tweak the organization's strategies and goals to make them more effective moving forward.

Furthermore, for an organization's goals to be achievable and measurable, the organization has to estimate the availability of its resources. When and where are the organization's financial resources being generated?

This question is especially important to fundraisers and the financial managers of the organization. How much funding will the organization need to implement the programming necessary to reach each of its goals?

If you are in a leadership role, you have the authority to define specific responsibilities for your staff and board. Additionally, each person needs to be informed of how long they will have to do what has been assigned. It is important that there is a mechanism for accountability in place so that everyone in your organization can see that all progress, or lack thereof, is being monitored effectively.

Once a fundraising team, determines its fundraising goals for the year, it is critical to find ways to measure those outcomes.

An organization must have benchmarks in place to help measure its progress toward meeting the goals set forth in its strategic plan. Having those guidelines will help the executive leadership report its success to the board, staff, donors, and other stakeholders. When I worked in academia, as both a department head and executive director, I was invited and expected to develop assessment criteria, within the strategic plan, which would allow me to clearly outline how different departments should function.

Along with the assistance of my staff at MCC Great Lakes, we came up with the following self-assessment tool to help staff measure their stated goals and objectives. We developed three levels of measurement and assigned scores to each level to help the staff identify which of their plans worked and which needed revision.

After board approval, the staff was provided with the three strategic plan assessment charts below: "Chart A," "Chart B," and "Chart C."

Chart A identifies the current level of success toward either a specific goal or the organization's overall strategic plan.

Chart B is a flowchart that works in tandem with Chart A. It is designed to show what course of action should be taken depending on the level of success achieved.

Chart C outlines your goals, activities, and timeline, in addition to showing who will do what.

For example, if your team's goal for the upcoming year is to raise $1000 more than it raised last year, the results will fall under one of the three following outcomes:

You may have been very successful, raising close to or over 100% of your annual goal, placing your team's performance at **level 3.**

You may have raised $750 more than the last year, or 75% success, which would place your team's performance at **level 2**.

Finally, your team may have raised only $500 more than last year, or less than 75% of your goal, which places your team's performance at **level 1**.

Although there are many ways to measure the progress towards reaching your organization's strategic goals, the following charts are models that worked well for us at MCC Great Lakes. It is in the best interest of every employee within an organization to utilize these charts, so there is a uniform process for interpreting successes as well as shortcomings.

Chart A

Three Levels of Success Measurement for Strategic Plan

Level 1	Level 2	Level 3
Below **75%** Success	**75 – 90%** Success	Above **90%** Success
Goals were not measurable	A couple of goals need sharpening	Goals and objectives measured as expected
Objectives were unrealistic	Objectives and activities could be improved	Objectives met criteria
Activities did not match goals and objectives	Activities need to be more aligned with objectives	Activities worked as expected
Goals overlap/redundant **Needs to be redone**	**Needs to be redone/revised**	**The plan needs no adjustment**

Strategic Planning

Chart B

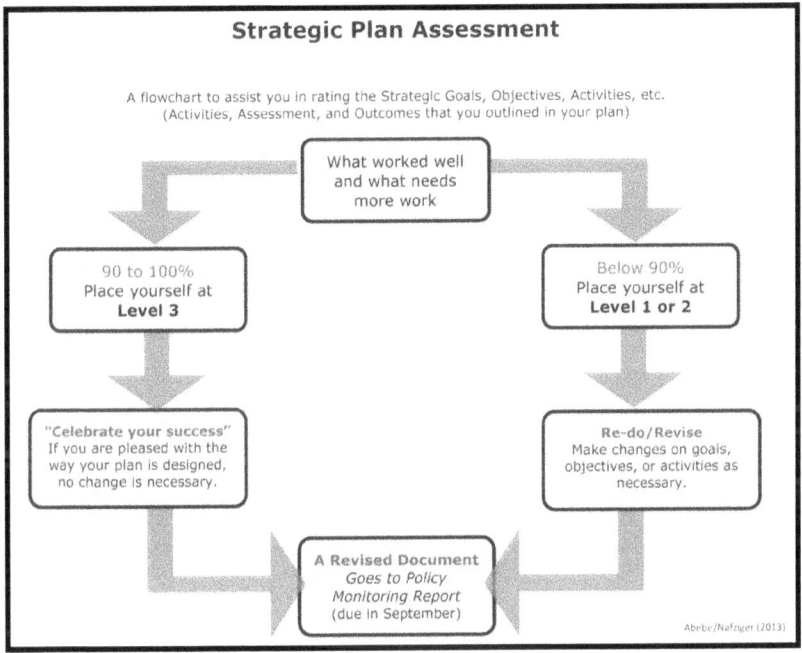

Chart C

Action Plan for Strategic Plan Assessment

Example Strategic Goal #1:
The University of Deder will increase its fundraising efforts by $1000 every year, using the current fiscal year's budget as its benchmark.

DATE	ACTIVITIES	ASSESSMENT METHODS	GOALS/OUTCOMES	RESPONSIBILITY
2019				
2020				
2021				
2022				
2023				

If your organization has a strategic plan, that plan should clearly state your organization's mission statement; its vision; an outline of its goals, objectives, and activities; and an overall timeline for the plan.

Peri Pakroo, author of the book *Starting & Building a Nonprofit: A Practical Guide (2013)*, expands on these components of a strategic plan. Those seeking further insight into the development of strategic plans are recommended to consult her book.

At the end of the strategic planning process, your team will have produced a document that outlines the resulting strategic plan. This strategic document is the living, breathing, and defining treatise that will guide your organization's actions over a set period of time.

Lastly your organization's strategic planning document needs to include a message to donors that clearly states what your organization plans to do and how it plans to do it. It is imperative to know and understand what motivates people to give. Donors give for many reasons, and I believe that the key reason is that they identify and resonate with your organization's inspired plan for the future.

As always, your organization's strategic plan will be more effective in articulating the direction of your organization when it is framed by a strong mission statement.

Qualities and Measures of Success in Fundraising

As I touched on in the previous chapter, success is hard to evaluate effectively unless it is measured. How does your organization's mission impact its outcomes? What benchmarks are used to measure success? Donors want to know this. If successes are measured, it is easier to communicate the organization's effectiveness to donors and thereby earn their support. As Gifford (2005) asserts: "It's tempting to keep doing what you've always done. But people's lives and donor's contributions are at stake.

"Success is to be measured not so much by the position that one has reached in life as by the obstacles which he has overcome trying to succeed."

Booker T. Washington

It's negligent to keep investing money in programs without proof they make a difference" (p. 31).

If a program is not doing well, this should also be measured and reported. Measurements of success can't be faked. A mission focused organization needs to be transparent.

Having benchmarks by which to measure effectiveness is essential. It helps an organization know what is and is not working. This enables the implementation of corrective action(s) so goals and objective are met within the desired timeline outlined in the strategic plan.

Max De Pree, in his book *Leading Without Power* (1997), says "Measurement is essential in an organization for several reasons. It's directly related to the health of the organization. It is directly connected to the way an organization can mature and grow" (p. 48).

Moreover, other experts in the field of measurement suggest that an organization's executive director should ask for input from his or her program staff before reporting any data, so he or she knows your program's outcome measurement.

When considering how to measure success, it is important to realize that not all organizations will define or reach success in the same way. Each organization can, and should, come up with their own metrics and benchmarks that fit the organization's mission.

On the other hand, many view measurement as less glamorous, tedious and impersonal. Deirdre Maloney, in her book *Building Nonprofit Momentum Through Better Business (2012),* highlights the following six important points to show why measurement is necessary for all your organization's programs.

Measurement:
- Proves your worth to stakeholders
- Shows that you are meeting your goals
- Allows you to make good decisions
- Illustrates your organization's commitment to excellence, strategy, and integrity
- Makes you stand out from your competition
- Can be done in-house, if needed, and within a fairly quick time frame. (p.246)

The purpose of employing metrics and benchmarks is simply a way to help an organization find ways to measure and determine how to best use their human and financial resources. Steven Rothschild suggests that providing qualitative and quantitative data to support an organization's measurements only strengthens the case for obtaining financial support.

Evaluation starts with fundraising goals. The evaluation process will help you to understand how much money needs to be raised and how much time there is to raise it. You need to do this first so that the funding is already in place and work may proceed unabated and according to the established budget and timeline for programmatic implementation.

Jeffery Haguewood, in his blog *HubSpot*, lists the following two critical metrics for measuring your fundraising performance:

1. You must be able to respond to your strategic goals. Did you raise what you said you would?
2. How about your return on investment? Was it worth spending what you spent on fundraising activities to secure what was raised in a given period of time? The money spent on resource generation must yield enough to cover your cost and advance your organization's' mission.

If your plan doesn't work, you change it. Everything we do in fundraising has to be evaluated to maintain effectiveness. We also need to be certain that our method of measurement is reliable.

Any program that an organization utilizes should be evaluated with regularity. There are countless activities to keep in mind when planning to fundraise for success In regard to evaluation and measurement, Maloney (2012), suggests five important things that fundraisers should remember, and as paraphrased bellow:

- Remember that you are acting as an ambassador for an organization and a cause that is important to you
- Remember that this organization needs money to get the mission done effectively
- Remember the people you serve
- Remember your commitment to whatever role you signed up for that put you in this position
- Remember that you are not asking for money for yourself; you are asking for money to help a cause, to advance a community. (p.176)

On the topic of measurement, and through applying Maloney's ideas, the following paraphrased six items are suggested as a framework to be considered as indicators of success.

First, success starts with the individual running the program. Do you like what you do? Are you excited about your role in fundraising? Being passionate about what you do is essential in attaining success.

Second, either the director or a designated associate monitors the progress being made relative to the fundraising goal and timeline. Follow-through procedures must be in place so any issues are quickly identified and corrective measures taken. Conformity to the strategic plan must be maintained.

Third, operating with sound ethical standards and integrity throughout the organization helps to ensure credibility. Donors are far more likely to support a reliable, ethical and fiscally sound organization.

Fourth, donors want the assurance that the support they offer is having an impact. Using effective stories, demonstrate the measured programmatic impact to the organization's supporters. Stories are one of the best forms of communication with donors and are a great way to update and inform.

Fifth, organizational values must be clear and demonstrable to those offering support. Let donors know that operational values are based on compassion and making a measurable difference in the lives of others.

Sixth, personal belief, devotion, and loyalty to the organization on the part of the board, leadership, and staff should be easily noticeable. Donors can tell if you are just working for pay or if you see your work as a calling, a commitment to making a difference.

Success doesn't happen by simply working hard but instead through modeling a spirit of optimism and resilience. Your commitment and passion for what you do says a lot about who you are.

Comments from survey respondents
(Research question 8)

Measuring success is hard to do for me. I like my organization and it is a well-respected and well supported. As an organization we have challenges to follow our strategic plan. As hard as we work, as much as we go through rituals of writing brochures, I wish we would apply them so we can measure what worked and what didn't. Yes, we do have all the mission statement, strategic plan and goals and objectives, but not much on the function. Would you tell us how to do it?

I am not a regular or professional fundraiser. I began 21 years ago as a CEO because of necessity, continued throughout the 21 years as a volunteer on top of my regular duties, and now in my "retired" time. I have never been paid a cent for my services. I have been involved with other volunteers also not paid. Together we must have raised more than six or seven million dollars for the organization. I have lost count. That gives us a sense of satisfaction that money cannot buy. But I am getting very tired.

Qualities and Measures of Success in Fundraising

Survey participants were asked how they measured their success as fundraisers on a scale from 1 to 10, with 10 as highest rating. Their responses are listed in rank order on the scale of importance:

- *When ethical standards are not compromised, but rather reinforced. (**130** points)*
- *When my values on compassion, care and social justice are affirmed. (**127** points)*
- *Success is measured by overall happiness and excitement at my job. (**122** points)*
- *When ethical standards are not compromised (**118** points)*
- *When effectively telling stories about work to donors ranked also forth with **118** on the scale of importance.*

Board Involvement in Fundraising

It is critical for board members to be actively involved in fundraising for their organization. The job of board members is not only to hire but also fire the executive director of their organization. Though that may have been true in the past, current methodology suggests that board members must have additional responsibilities.

    It is common today for board members to be reluctant about getting involved in multiple areas of their organizations. This is unfortunate, because board members have the potential to be, and often are, contributors to many facets of their organizations.

> "It's not just about being able to write a check. It's being able to touch somebody's life."
>
> **Oprah Winfrey**

To be effective, however, board members should not shy away from getting involved in identifying new fundraising opportunities to thanking donors.

Board members are often busy people, but, leading with action is substantially more effective than leading with words. McNott (2008) puts it bluntly,

"The three Gs, for nonprofit board members: 'Give, Get, Get off'...However, it's more important that 100% of them are giving as generously as they are able." (p.85)

Board members can and should, according to their individual gifts and skills, get involved in the organization's fundraising efforts in one of the following three ways:

First, board members are expected to offer personal financial contributions to their organizations. They should also actively solicit financial support from those in their social network.

Second, board members should identify prospective donors with capacity and affinity, and, when they can, facilitate communication with these people.

Third, board members should assist in thanking the organization's generous donors by making phone calls and sending thank you notes. It should be part of an organization's strategy to foster board engagement in all aspects of fundraising.

Gail Perry, author of *Fired-UP Fundraising, Turn Board Passion into Action* (2007), has developed a Checklist of Basic Fundraising Requirements of Board Members.

Some of the activities described are not new and are routinely performed by the board members of many organizations. However, some of what Perry describes is not yet common practice for board members. After consulting with Perry, I have summarized and paraphrased her expectations for nonprofit board members as follows.

She suggests that nonprofit organizations adapt this checklist of basic fundraising requirements based on their specific fundraising programs:

- We require all board members to make an annual gift to the best of his or her ability
- We expect 100% board participation for our public events
- We expect board members to bring their friends and contacts to our events
- We expect board members to help thank the organization's donors
- We expect board members to help make new friends and contacts for the organization

- We expect board members to, when appropriate, ask for contributions
- We expect board members to know and support the fundraising plan
- We expect board members to be sure that the current fundraising program has adequate internal and external support. (p.161)

Suffice it to say, board engagement in fundraising and the cultivation of relationships with donors is imperative to the success of nonprofit organizations in the current philanthropic landscape.

I was privileged to serve on the United Way board. When I joined the board, it was a given for every board member to donate. We were also expected to get involved in the annual fundraising drive at each of our workplaces in order to raise money for the United Way.

Solomon Belette, another expert in the field of philanthropy and the director of the Sanford Institute of Philanthropy at John F. Kennedy University, offers the following three guidelines that nonprofit organizations can establish to supercharge their boards:

One: Board members have a fiduciary duty to steer their organization toward a sustainable future.

Two: Board members have ethical and legal duties to protect the organization and its reputation from exposure to risks and liabilities.

Three: Board members are, in partnership with the organization's leadership, responsible for framing and developing sound policies, implementing best practices in finance and human resources, and serving as a check and balance to others in the organization with regards to decision making.

It is also important to recognize that while the board of directors may have many roles, it is key that members of an organization understand the difference between the roles of board members and the role of the executive director.

John and Miriam Carver, well known authors admired for their development of the policy model for boards of directors, state in Carver's guide *The CEO Role Under Policy Governance (1997)* that, "The board's job is to decide the goals, and the chief executive officer's job to determine the means to achieve the board's [ends.]" Here, Carver draws a line that distinguishes the board's job from that of the executive director. In addition to the financial contributions that board members are expected to make to their organizations,

Carver makes a critical point about their relationship with the executive director.

"In the long run, boards taking responsibility for board effectiveness is the only path to governance integrity and the only foundation for a superior board–CEO relationship." (p.19)

Carver's cut and dry governance organizational model aims to minimize confusion between the responsibilities of an organization's executive director and its board.

In Carver's model, the responsibilities and job descriptions for the board and the executive director are clear.

For example, Carver simply states that an organization's board should be responsible for hiring only one person, the executive director, who will, in turn, be responsible for hiring the rest of the organization's staff. Many believe this to be helpful in reducing corruption, particularly by board members, in the hiring and promoting of staff. On fundraising, Carver (2002) simply states that, "board engagement in finding resources is critical to continued existence and success." (p. 467)

In sum, so long as they are active and engaged, nonprofit board members can be important to the life of the organization they serve. As with any person within an organization, each board member provides different gifts and skills to support the organization's staff and overall efforts. It is incredibly helpful to an organization when each board member uses their unique skills to aid the efforts of the organization in any and every way they can.

Comments from survey respondents (Research question 10)

We are working on this. Our board members, over the past 5 years, have become more involved with fundraising.

This is very important for the organization and our success, but no one wants to talk about it openly. I hope we will keep focusing on this.

Thank you for contacting me to participate. It is a privilege working with you on this project. I hope your work is less academic and more real-world and hands on experiential report.

Some of our board members are very engaged and giving their time, resources and I appreciate what they stand for. Others are there simply to experience being board members at the organization. You can tell they are new at this, and I can tell they do respect what we do and yet not much wisdom to offer.

I am very much for the board involvement in the life of our organization, as long as they are aware of their boundaries and responsibilities. I appreciate their commitment and sacrifice.

Listening to Donors

When fundraisers communicate with potential donors, it is important that they pay attention to what the potential donor is saying. Often fundraisers underestimate the degree to which they truly listen to donors. Good listening requires that you are fully engaged so that you can respond to a donor or potential donor's questions correctly. James M. Kouzes and Barry Z. Posner, in their book *The Truth about Leadership (2010),* wrote: "When you listen, when you hear, and when you truly understand the needs of your constituents, you will connect with them in way that an out-of-touch leader cannot." (p. 65)

> "Every intersection in the road of life is an opportunity to make a decision, and at some time to only listen."
>
> **Duke Ellington**

Giving donors the opportunity to respond to what they hear is critical. A fundraiser must always give donors the chance to ask questions and to clarify possible misunderstandings. It is also important for a fundraiser to pay attention to topics repeatedly addressed by a current or potential donor. This will give you the opportunity to tailor your appeal or solicitation approach to the current or potential donor's personality, passions, and interests.

When it comes to asking for donations, there are several ways to do this. Occasionally, simply telling a donor the mission of your organization and describing its needs is enough to solicit a donation. If you know, or have access to, a published story about your organization's accomplishments, be sure to share it. Peter Brinckerhoff, in his book *Smart Stewardship for Nonprofits: Making the Right Decision in Good Times and Bad* (2012), encourages us to "tell the mission stories at every meeting" (p. 56). Even better, if you can, have someone working in the field for your organization share a first-hand account of work that has achieved a positive impact. All these things may help to convince a potential donor to offer support, since they make your organization stand out as interesting, effective, and caring.

On a broader level, if your organization is honest and successful, it may draw media attention. Ideally, a significant portion of your organization's publicity will come from local and regional news outlets. It is imperative that your organization capitalizes on any opportunity for positive media exposure. Getting your organization's donors to be excited about what you do plays a big part in attracting positive media attention.

While I worked at MCC Great Lakes, we had an understanding among the fundraising team about how to communicate with donors. Following the formerly mentioned Thomas Wolf's suggestion, donors that provided a high level of support to MCC Great Lakes were given personalized acknowledgement. Each of our staff would identify high-level donors in their region and let me know when I could contact those donors by phone, letter, or in person. We did this to acknowledge the donor, thank them for their gifts, and to give the donor an opportunity to ask about our organization's work.

From reaching out to these donors, I have collected many stories that are encouraging and inspiring. As Parker Palmer, author of *A Hidden Wholeness* (2004), argues: "We find common bonds in the shared details of the human journey, not in the divergent conclusions we draw from those details." (p. 124)

The following are some of my personal favorite stories from my time at MCC Great Lakes:

A Story of Trust

I once phoned the home of a couple who had been supporting MCC for many years. The husband thanked me for contacting them and said to me: "We never got calls from the organization to thank us. They probably tried and never got through, because we're not home a lot. We appreciate your call, however, to call or to write to thank us is not necessary, and we do not expect it. We know what you are doing, and we have no doubt that the money we give goes where it should, and we are happy."

A Story of Compassion

I contacted another family who had been donating a lot of money to MCC. When I told the family that I wanted to meet over lunch to thank them for their support, they welcomed the invitation, and we met at a local restaurant. At the end of our visit, the family told me that they gave for two reasons: because they were able to do so, and because MCC stood out as an organization that they highly respected. "Please continue what you do, and please know that we do not need encouragement to give. We are committed to stay with the organization. Keep up the good work, and blessings to you and your staff."

A Story of Commitment

This story focuses on another couple that were known as "high-level donors" at MCC Great Lakes. After greeting them, this couple told me that they had been carefully watching the activities of MCC. They said that they continued to be impressed by what they saw. They were convinced that their support made a difference. "Thank you for contacting us, but there is no need to call or write more. However, let us know when you organize a public meeting in our area so we can come and hear stories."

A Story of Confidence

This story is one that particularly touched me. I had known this donor couple for many years; our children even attended the same school. The husband had on several occasions, invited me to join him for breakfast, a tradition we repeated often during the fall and spring of each year. In addition to being my friend, this man is highly connected with several community organizations and supports many charities. He knows a lot about fundraising, and I always saw him as my mentor.

At the end of each of our breakfast meetings, he would go back to his office, and soon after arriving at his office, would send me a copy of a freshly-sent email to his accountant, instructing him to send money to the MCC Great Lakes Office. I always followed up his messages with a thank you letter. This went on for some time, and he also lent me a book on fundraising.

I believe that it was during the third year of our breakfast meetings and his generous gifts that my friend told me that he would like to do more for MCC, something in addition to his regular gifts. He asked me to identify a project that he could support beyond his regular donations.

After consulting with my fundraising team, I sent my friend a list of three projects, along with each project's estimated costs, for him to choose. After a couple of weeks, he sent us a check to completely fund one of the projects.

A Story of Affirmation

This story involves a high-level donor and longtime friend of mine, one who I had known since we attended college together. Since I was traveling near his home and had another appointment in his area, I contacted his office and made an appointment to travel to his hometown to meet with him for lunch and to thank him for his support. After our lunch, he gave me a big check to be used toward a project he wished to support. My friend's affirmation of our work at MCC and his continued commitment to that work meant more than he could imagine. For a supporter to say to us, "we appreciate what you do," is one thing, but to also affirm what you do by writing a big check to our organization says much more than the gift itself: It has the potential to boost our morale, our confidence in what we do, and also affirms our mission.

While many of the donors I contacted said that they did not need to be thanked, they were all overjoyed at MCC's gratitude. Because many donors do not expect such gratitude, it is even more powerful for them when they are thanked.

While these are all positive stories, I also have stories, although not many, where donors contacted our office to tell us that they would no longer support what we do for some philosophical or political reason.

Even in these cases, we at MCC Great Lakes would make the conscious decision to not cut off communication. Instead, we continued to keep in contact with these donors with the hope that they would change their minds.

Regardless of the state of a donor-fundraiser relationship, fundraisers must do their best to connect with donors. At a time when fewer and fewer people are giving, nonprofit organizations need to steward the donors they have.

Why People Give

Why do donors give? The short answer is because they are asked to give. I would also like to believe that donors give because of their belief in an organization's mission. But perhaps most importantly, donors give because they want to give.

Studies have shown that people give not because they feel like they have to, but instead because they have the desire to give back. The other reason donors give can be that the culture we live in may dictate what we do with our wealth. For those of us living in the often-affluent Western culture, giving is very much a common practice that is encouraged.

> "Love grows by giving. The love we give away is the only love we keep. The only way to retain love is to give it away."
>
> **Elbert Hubbard**

It is important to acknowledge that Americans are generally givers that like to help those in need.

Most of us are aware of the blessing that comes with giving. I am fond of the Booker T. Washington quote that says: "Those who are happiest are those who do the most for others." Showing that a love for giving is not unique to one generation, Maya Angelou, who was born almost a decade after Booker T. Washington passed away, wrote: "When we give cheerfully and accept gratefully, everyone is blessed."

The aforementioned Marshall McNott spent 40 years in nonprofit leadership and raised millions in that time. McNott, in his book *Nonprofit Nonsense & Common Sense (2008)*, says: "Almost all of the world's great religions encourage their followers to donate their time and money to help the less fortunate (p.1).

Similarly, those of us working at faith-based organizations are familiar with Francis of Assisi's prayer that goes, "for it is in giving that we receive."

Why else do donors give? Typically, donors want to give when they know an organization affects change with the donations they receive. Donors want to avoid giving donations to organizations that spend exorbitant amounts on overhead expenses. We understand that donors want to give to organizations that spend a maximum of 35% of donations on overhead costs. Some experts in the field even suggest that donors prefer when overhead costs do not exceed 20% of an organization's budget.

Many others see their donations as an investment, especially when they see evidence that the support they offer is making a difference in the lives of others. Some donors would like to see their donations reach as many people as possible. Alex Daniels calls this a code of transparency to this generation.

For some donors, it is important to be able to see results first-hand. These donors would like to see pictures or be taken on a learning tour to see what the organization is doing. I have been told by past participants that Mennonite Economic Development Association (MEDA) is an excellent example of how to run learning tours.

For others, it is important that donors see a balanced annual budget. Do not overlook or underestimate the value of a well-prepared annual report. Some organizations have begun calling the annual report an "impact report" in order to positively position the work accomplished. It is industry standard among nonprofit organizations to provide a financial summary in a pie-chart form to show how an organization ended their fiscal year. A summarized financial report will help you to build trust with your organization's donors.

Some donors give for the tax benefits (charitable deductions) that making contributions affords them. It can also help encourage donors to give when they understand that someone will match their donation, as this makes donors feel like they a have a larger impact. Furthermore, faculty member Sara Konrath of Indiana University-Purdue University Indianapolis and Femida Handy of the University of Pennsylvania, in their online blog "The Conversation" (2017), identified "being asked" as a main reason for why people give. In fact, they pointed out that more than 85% of charitable donors gave because someone asked them to. In addition to being asked, Konrath and Handy, in the same post, suggested the following five main reasons for why people give charitably: trust, altruism, social pressure, taxes, and egoism.

While reading *Network for Good, The Nonprofit Marketing Blog*, I found a 2015 article titled "How To Get Donations: 14 Reasons Why People Donate." Here are some of the top listed reasons for why donors give:

- They are asked to give
- They are emotionally moved by a story they heard

- They want to help
- They want to change someone's life
- They want to feel a sense of togetherness with those in need
- They want to memorialize someone with a gift
- They have a tradition of giving
- They want to support charity
- They want to have or maintain a good social image
- They want to give back
- They want to be a role model

When looking at this and other lists describing why people give, the motivations are quite similar. The one thing that is clear is that philanthropy is significant to donors, and the reason that a donor chooses to give is unique to each donor.

It is very important for board members, staff, and fundraisers to know that donors will continue to give if they have developed meaningful relationships with the organization and its staff.

These responses from survey participants disclose a very interesting and still important ranking worth noting when asked why donors give: **(Research question 15)**

- *Donating to "make a difference in someone's life" rated as the top response at 128 points*
- *Donating because of an organization's clear and coherent mission came in second at 120 points*
- *That at least 65% of an organization's funds go to programs came in third at 87 points*
- *Benefits, such as tax deduction, came in fourth at 83 points*

Legacy Donors

Thus far, all the activities and types of gifts I have discussed involve lifetime giving on the part of donors. But there is another form of support that needs to be mentioned, because it may be transformational for a charitable organization.

    I am referring to gifts that come through an individual's will or trust. These gifts are sometimes referred to as estate gifts or bequests. Regardless of the size of an estate, a person may choose to pass on their values by deciding to leave legacy gifts to their favorite charities after their lifetime. Some of the gifts will be restricted for a specific purpose or

> "The real measure of your wealth is how much you'd be worth if you lost all your money."
>
> **Unknown Author**

program, while others are undesignated and may be used where they are needed most.

Occasionally, donors will let the organization know that they have made a provision for the charity through their future planning, but it is far more common for the charities to not be informed until after the donor's lifetime.

For a great many organizations, the need for immediate operating funds is of utmost importance. Therefore, little staff time is directed towards the recruitment and securing of legacy gifts that will come in the future. That's because it is hard to know when, or if, those gifts will ever be realized. In this section, I will touch on the important characteristics of legacy gifts.

During my tenure as director, I was very impressed anytime a donor was proactive in their planning and thought enough of MCC Great Lakes to provide a future gift. In most cases, though, legacy gifts take years to mature. It is not uncommon for 10 to 20 or more years to go by before the legacy gift is received.

For this reason, bequests provide an exciting and unexpected blessing each time they arrive. At MCC Great Lakes, whenever we received one of these gifts, I would pause and ask myself what we did to deserve such a generous blessing. For MCC, being included in a donor's crowning act of stewardship was a source of pure joy. These gifts provided a boost to our annual budget and lifted staff morale. Given the unique nature of legacy gifts, I would always try to learn the background story of why a donor chose to leave a gift to MCC Great Lakes. I wanted to learn something from each story to help me be more effective in my contacts with other donors going forward.

Most of the time, donors that leave a gift from their will or trust do so because they want to make difference and affirm the values that they held dear during their lifetime. One of the gifts we received came from a family, from whom I happened to know some of their distant relatives. Over the years, a meaningful relationship had been developed with this family by my predecessors and staff at MCC.

Their commitment to getting to know and relate to this family is what ultimately led them to plan for their eventual gift. Because these gifts are usually the result of a donor's long-term association with MCC, I knew that it was the result of the influence and cultivation of many staff members over the years.

It is possible, however, for a bequest to come from someone with no obvious connection to the organization. It takes investigative work to uncover a connection, but when the story comes together, it is truly gratifying.

Some of our supporters are very private people, and they prefer to do their giving in an unsung and quiet manner, and that needs to be respected. I was fortunate, during my time at MCC, to acknowledge the receipt of several legacy gifts. They were large and small, restricted and unrestricted, simple and complex.

The gifts took on many forms, but these are the most common: being named as a beneficiary of a retirement plan, being named to receive a gift directly from a will or trust, or naming MCC to receive memorial or honorary gifts.

It is important for me to note that legacy gifts involve legal and tax considerations that the donor pursued with their professional advisors. I always made it clear to a donor that I could not offer legal or tax advice. They needed to receive their own counsel. I could provide specific information such as our recommended bequest language, our tax ID number, and any guidelines we had in place for the establishment of named or permanent funds, which would support the organization in perpetuity.

I will always remember a personal letter that I received from an executor informing me that a family had left a substantial gift to our organization. In this particular case, I was asked by the executor to keep this gift confidential. Furthermore, I was instructed to not share the news of the gift with the media. Coming from a background in higher education, this was a departure from what I had observed as being the norm. In higher education, it seems as if monumental gifts are made public and the donor is recognized in some way.

A donor's wish to remain anonymous must be honored. Every gift, no matter the size, was important to us, and we accepted each one with gratitude and recognized the donors appropriately.

There are many kinds of donors: from first-time givers to long-term committed donors who sustain the program. It is important to realize that donors who stick with you will move through stages, and as a result, their commitment to your organization may increase as they learn more and engage with the staff.

Often, it is an organization's clear and effective mission statement that attracts first-time donors. It takes the building of a meaningful relationship over time for them to become life-long givers.

It is truly special when you find those donors who are committed to support your organization's mission, no matter what. They will be much more likely to stay with your organization because of your ongoing contact and friendship with them. If a legacy gift is planned, it will most likely happen because of the donor's long-term association with key staff members from within the organization.

In putting together an approach to encourage legacy gifts from within your existing support base, you should target those donors who give consistently over a long period of time. The size of their gifts is not nearly as important as the regularity of their gifts when it comes to identifying legacy gift prospects.

Once the prospects have been identified, the staff member charged with exploring legacy gifts with them will first need to develop a degree of comfort in bringing up the subject. One consultant suggested the following language to use when meeting with a prospect: "Mr. and Mrs. donor, you have regularly given to MCC Great Lakes for many years. That is a wonderful track record of support, and I thank you. From my experience, it has been donors, like you, who support us so faithfully and that have also taken the extraordinary step of including MCC Great Lakes as a beneficiary, in one way or another, of your estate plan."

This is where you wait and listen for their response. If they say "yes," you might invite them to share what they have in mind. If they say "no," you can offer to provide additional information for them to consider. It is a non-threatening way to start the conversation.

A number of us at MCC Great Lakes, in collaboration with a local financial institution, worked on implementing estate planning as a service to our supporters.

I want to emphasize the value of acknowledgment and gratitude on the part of everyone in your organization that has contact with your donors. Everything your organization does depends on having generous donors. It is critical that all staff members realize that these donors are the lifeblood of your organization and that, their friendships with these donors are essential to your organization. You do not want to lose these donors or the regular contact your organization has with them that results in major giving.

None of the legacy gifts MCC Great Lakes received when I was executive director were given because of what I did. They were given because of the work done by those building important friendships donors well before I got there. Ongoing relationships pay off, trust pays off, and most of all, staying in touch with your donors pays off. Hopefully, the seeds that I planted with donors during my time will bear fruit for the current staff, from now and into the future.

The following action plan may help your organization to retain its legacy donors: Firstly, stay in touch with all your donors. Secondly, remember to report back to them to ask for their feedback. Better yet, consider inviting them to join you in the field to see some of your programs in action. Learning tours will help your organization's donors to develop a personal connection with your organization. As mentioned before, we can look to MEDA as an example of an organization that has consistently provided good experiences for its donors.

It is critical to pay attention to all the donors of your organization. Some give a lot, some give less, and some may volunteer their time. Regardless, donors give as they are able. What might be a relatively small gift to your organization may have been a significant gift for a donor. In all cases, studies on fundraising indicate that it is all about relationships.

A relationship may be with an individual or a group, but what matters is that you know them well and that you maintain a relationship with them. Research shows that 78% or more of charitable funding will come from individuals. Therefore, individual donors and your relationships with them will likely be more significant from a fundraising perspective than the organization's relationship with foundations and/or corporations.

The importance of nurturing relationships with your donors was the point of an article published in the *Chronicle of Philanthropy* (2018), in which author Nicole Wallace asserts that, because fewer people are giving, charities need to hold on to the donors. Do not take your regular donors for granted, you may not see them again.

First-Time Donors

We've already established the importance of building up a dedicated donor base. With that said, it is crucial that fundraisers recognize that every impassioned, longtime donor was once a first-time donor themselves, one that might have even been on the fence about donating to your organization.

When considering a potential first-time donor, don't assume that the donor fully understands your organization. Before meeting with a potential first-time donor, prepare a welcome packet that includes key information about your organization.

> "Success is the result of perfection, hard work, learning from failure, loyalty, and persistence."
>
> **Colin Powell**

Moreover, your organization must be intentional about how it approaches first-time donors. Instead of deciding how to meet with potential donors on the fly, your organization should treat each potential donor as a unique case, just as every potential donor is a unique individual.

Your organization should select the appropriate staff or board member to meet or correspond with each potential donor. Additionally, you and your organization must have some level of knowledge about each potential donor. If you have a basic understanding of a potential donor, your odds of effectively communicating with them increases dramatically. If you do your homework, you will know the appropriate amount of money to ask for from each donor and which projects to pitch. Knowing your potential donors will also help you to identify the right time to ask for a donation.

After a potential donor gives for the first time and becomes a donor, ensure that you offer thanks. Display gratitude to all donors. First-time donors especially will enjoy thank you notes and phone calls as this demonstrates that their gifts don't go unnoticed.

Whenever you thank a donor, tailor the thank you specifically to that donor. In doing so, consider your relationship to the donor and the donor's level of knowledge about your organization.

The following is the story of how a thank you letter touched the heart of a first-time donor:

A Story of Gratitude

We will call this person "David," though that is not his real name. I ran into David at an event shortly after I decided to write this book. David and I spent some time talking about our lives, and I told him that I was writing a book about nonprofit fundraising. He said that he was excited for me, and he volunteered to share this story about his experience as a first-time donor.

In the 1970s, David was an international student attending a small American liberal arts college on scholarship. Upon graduating from college, David decided to attend graduate school.

About a month or two into his time at graduate school, David unexpectedly received a letter from his undergraduate alma mater asking him for a donation. David was stunned and confused by the letter he received.

In some ways, David felt honored and respected that someone had thought of him as someone important enough to be asked for a donation. On the other hand, he felt ashamed for he had no money to give to the college that had given him the opportunity to earn his degree.

David began to ponder the idea of donating. Later, he told a couple of close friends about the letter he had received, and he asked for advice on how to respond. At the time David received the letter from his alma mater, he had thought a donation meant a large sum of money, something solicited from rich people, not from a poor grad student like him. After a time spent struggling to figure out what to do, David decided to send what little he had in his pocket to his alma mater. Along with his donation, David wrote a letter to his alma mater that explained his financial situation: "I wish to help, but I am not in a position to do so at the moment."

He felt so bad about sending his letter without a significant donation. Nonetheless, he enclosed in an envelope what he thought was an embarrassing amount of money and mailed it to his alma mater, fearing that he may not hear from them again.

To his surprise, David received a response letter from his former school about a week later. To his astonishment, it was a thank you letter. A portion of the letter read: "We thank you so much for your generous support. Your gift will make a difference in the lives of other students."

He was once again flabbergasted, and he began telling his friends about the thank you letter and about how proud he was to receive it, despite donating what he described as nothing. David told me that this story was the beginning of his persisting and meaningful connection with his alma mater.

David's story is a good example of why every donor is important. It shows how any gift could be the beginning of a long-term donor relationship. Most of all, David's story is an example of the meaningfulness of gratitude, especially with first-time donors. This true story can be a reminder of the persistence and care fundraisers put into their work. What we say matters, and a small beginning may lead to a big success.

Comments from survey respondents
(Research question 13)

We are very staff-driving in our fundraising. In the past, capital campaigns have had a volunteer steering committee, but we have not utilized a committee for about 12 years.

I write a personal thank you on the letter if they are recurring donors or have given a specific amount.

Section 3

A Framework for Action: Showing Results and Building Trust

- Developing an Organizational Plan for Fundraising
- Communication
- Empowering Those Being Served
- Endowment
- Accountability

Developing an Organizational Plan for Fundraising

Apart from an organization's overall strategic plan, it is necessary to have a fundraising plan in place that evaluates what is needed for its day-to-day operations. Furthermore, an organization should be aware of any philanthropic trends, with regards to its current sources of income. It should also think about any new avenues of support that could be explored. Think of the future: How are your organization's programs expected to change in the upcoming years? What would be the resulting financial impact of those changes?

> "Always plan ahead. It wasn't raining when Noah built the ark."
>
> **Richard Cushing**

It is possible, with the help of an organization's accounting and fundraising staffs, to map out the organization's fundraising goals. When doing so, it is important to always include both the organization's overhead and direct costs.

Any nonprofit organization should do all it can to ensure that as much of the resources generated as possible are directed to its programs. After all, that *is* the mission and why the organization exists. There are the ongoing costs associated with keeping an organization up and running and ready to address the needs that arise. One of the recurring comments I heard from the staff of organizations similar to MCC is that many donors step up and respond when a natural disaster or newsworthy event takes place, but they soon disappear and do not respond to subsequent appeals for annual or sustaining support.

There are costs that must be covered to keep the organization's structure strong and prepared to respond quickly when major events occur. It's the costs associated with long-term recovery, sustainable development, and program implementation, which happen long after the headlines have disappeared, that require critical ongoing support generated through the organization's fundraising efforts.

At the end of the day, an organization needs to be aware of how it aims to achieve its fundraising goals. At the end of each quarter, an organization should take the time to analyze what it has been doing well and what it needs to do better: What programs need to be reshaped or require more time or more resources? Is the fundraising staff structured so that all areas of philanthropy, such as prospecting, the annual fund, major donors, legacy donors, and stewardship are being addressed?

A successful organization will systematically evaluate its fundraising plan so that all resource generation related activity is properly focused. In doing so, it commits to being a good steward of the support that is given. Ultimately, it enables the organization to achieve maximum impact towards accomplishing its mission.

Comments from survey respondents (Research question 19)

> *Yes, but all of our development officers are "contact" people. We are all always on the lookout for ways to advance the mission of the organization, so anyone can become a conduit through which donors connect. I am simply the person who coordinates all of our development activity.*

Communication

Too often, we communicate without truly understanding one another. Effective communication between two parties involves presenting ideas that are communicated simply and thoughtfully. The involved parties should not be attempting to score points or win an argument.

In the world of fundraising, the purpose of communication is to create greater understanding and to convey the organization's mission and purpose to others. Regular communication with donors is at the core of what makes fundraisers successful. You need to be informed of key aspects of

> "The single biggest problem in communication is the illusion that it has taken place."
>
> **George Bernard Shaw**

your organization and whether its focus is local or international.

I have already noted that it will be a connection with the organization's mission that first catches a donor's attention. But most donors will want to go beyond that and learn more. Questions donors might ask include: "Where is the organization operating?" "How long have you been active in this particular work?" "What has been accomplished to date?"

"What are the plans going forward?" These are all legitimate questions, and your organization's fundraising staff should be prepared to answer them.

The question, then, is how? Donors will have different preferences for how they like to receive information. Some will prefer to read printed materials, while others will want to be contacted via email. Many donors will appreciate "old fashioned" notes and letters. Some would be happy to receive information through church bulletins, and still others prefer to get their information from social media. A carefully thought out communication strategy, which targets different audiences, will yield the best results.

Maintaining a highly skilled communication department makes the process of staying in touch with donors much easier. The communication team should produce consistent messaging for the organization. As a result, having staff members who are well-equipped to generate high-quality brochures, edit letters, maintain an up-to-date presence on the web, and handle contacts with local media outlets are a critical part of any organization. They make a big difference in effectively communicating what your organization has accomplished to the broader public.

Perhaps more than anything, an effective communication department helps its organization to form meaningful connections with its donors by helping provide a consistent message through fundraising literature or through "talking points" provided to those making oral presentations. According to Alex Daniels, the number one skill a successful fundraiser should have is the ability to use good judgment in their communication with donors.

As a fundraiser, your persistence on delivering a truthful, positive, and consistent message, as prepared by your communication department, will greatly augment your ability to build a donor's trust in your organization.

Although it takes time, building trust is a critical component of the relationship between fundraisers and donors. Conversely, losing that trust can happen much more and can have a devastating effect on an organization. In the world of fundraising, it is in the best interest of your team to maintain trust. If you say you are going to do something, do it and show the results.

From my experience, the best way to build trust with donors is by being a person of integrity. This means being truthful in what you share and not stretching or misrepresenting the facts. If you don't know the answer to a question, admit it, and commit to finding out the answer and getting back to the donor in a timely manner.

Donors pay close attention to what fundraisers say. They keep track of whether the organization delivers on its promises. From the first encounter onwards, communicate your intentions as clearly and as honestly as possible.

Let your donors know what their donations will accomplish. Be prepared to respond to a donor's request for an update or a request to see evidence of how their support made a difference in lives of others.

There will inevitably come a time when, perhaps for reasons outside of the organization's control, a particular program initiative will not go as expected. I always found it to be a best practice to be proactive in reaching out to donors who have a special interest in that work and let them know what happened. When you do that, they will be much more likely to be understanding.

A fundraiser must be ready to respond to a donor's inquiry for financial statements or other supporting information that demonstrates the fiscal strength of your organization. A donor might ask for data regarding the number of volunteers within your organization or the percentage of your board and staff who contribute financially to the very mission they serve. If your staff and board of directors do not support your organization, it is less likely that a donor will choose to support it. This is where your ability to effectively convey your organization's stories becomes critical.

Sharing your organization's success stories is a great technique for building a donor's interest and trust in your organization. If you plan to tell a story about your organization, be sure to tell an effective story that is closely aligned to the donor's particular area of interest. I found that the best stories usually involved works of compassion.

Try to make the donation process as smooth as possible for each donor. When working with a major donor, utilize the information available from your own donor data base as well as what can be learned from public sources to build a case for that specific donor. Challenge the donor by either asking for a specific dollar amount or by providing a gift range for the donor to consider. Give them a series of program choices from which they could choose to donate. This makes the donor-fundraiser interaction more direct and sets a clear expectation for both parties.

It can be tempting to focus almost all of your efforts on working with high-level donors. If you work one-on-one with this group, you will have the opportunity to get them excited about and involved in your organization's mission. This is a good thing, but this is also where a fundraiser must utilize good judgment: Research shows that organizations have to be careful to not depend too heavily on high-level donors. It is best to have a broad base of support.

Our communication with donors must be centered around addressing the needs of many around the world. My staff at MCC Great Lakes would often hear me say that we had no product to offer, only our mission, which is focused on solving problems. In the words of Buck Rogers, who was a marketing executive at IBM "...at IBM, we don't sell products -we sell solutions".

Let our supporters know that because of their gifts we are able to solve many problems.

Having the ability to effectively communicate with our donors was a great luxury provided by our communication staff. When you have an effective communication staff, your odds of being successful in presenting your organization's mission will be greatly enhanced.

In my time at MCC Great Lakes, our storytelling brochures and letter writing all relied on our communications department. There were many occasions when we would not have enjoyed success in our work with donors without the effective materials provided by our talented staff.

I was fortunate to have had the privilege of working with an incredible communications coordinator during my years at MCC Great Lakes. This person knew what to do, when to do it, and was great at crafting the language I needed when presenting proposals to our donors. It was this person, along with other passionate communicators, that enabled me to be consistently successful in communicating our organization's mission to others.

Empowering Those Being Served

None of us started life without help from someone else. Whether we recognize it or not, the wisdom, compassion, and gentle mentorship from others helped shape us into who we are today. We all benefited through receiving help from others. We have been encouraged and supported by those we call co-workers, friends, and acquaintances.

Shortly before writing this book, I attended an annual church conference where I learned about the many fundraising activities underway within our denominational churches.

> "How far you go in life depends on our being tender with the young, compassionate with the aged, sympathetic with the striving, and tolerant of the weak and strong. Because someday in life you will have been all of these."
>
> **George Washington Carver**

At the conference, it was reported by a number of people that churches were involved in fundraising for over sixty different developmental projects around the world. Among the projects mentioned in their report were:
- Church planting
- Schools and colleges
- Community health centers
- Water development projects
- Community development projects

Not only do these churches support the initial brick and mortar building projects, but they also continue to support the project's ongoing operating costs and program functions. This is not a recent development, as churches have supported many of these projects for fifty to sixty years.

In the spirit of collaboration and outreach, the sharing of resources between churches and nonprofit organizations should be welcomed and encouraged. Nonprofit organizations should appreciate what churches are doing and see them as partners.

Churches and nonprofits often have similar missions and objectives for their projects, but they also face some of the same challenges. Ensuring the sustainability of projects is a challenge for both churches and nonprofits.

Both need to come together to consider the long-term impact of a community becoming financially independent and less reliant on the aid that they had been receiving. This, if not managed with care and mutual understanding, can unintentionally end up creating a situation consisting of power and control, dependency, and self-determination issues.

Perhaps it is time to rethink the way organizations and the communities they support work together. Those on the receiving end of support should view themselves as equal partners in long-term community development. One avenue for accomplishing this is to teach fundraising skills to members of the supported community so that they are trained to educate and solicit funding from local wealthy individuals and businesses.

As highlighted in a recent *A Common Place* (2019) magazine, independence and sustainable community development is one of MCC's missions. To that end, Lynn Longenecker, education coordinator for MCC, sees education to be more than literacy, basic reading and writing, and math.

"...Education is all of these layers that empower a person to have a voice and have an active role in defining their life and contributing to their community." (p.16-17)

From the perspective of fundraisers, it is necessary for nonprofit organizations to be cognizant of the hardships confronting the people and communities being served. The people that fundraisers raise support for around the world are no less human than the fundraisers. They simply happen to have been victims of an event or political climate that impacted their lives without warning.

If your organization's mission is compassion, it is important to treat those whom your organization supports with respect and dignity. People we consider refugees, people in need, and displaced people all wish for and deserve dignity and respect. Consequentially, if an organization wants to empower those they serve, they will work to enable the independence of those people, for attaining independence generates respect and dignity.

The Office of the United Nations High Commissioner for Human Rights reported that at the end of 2016, there were 65.6 million refugees in the world. As nonprofit organizations and churches work together to raise funds to support these displaced people, we must not forget their right to dignity and respect. Like us, they are human.

Anyone who has ever taken an introductory level psychology course will remember

Maslow's hierarchy of needs, which describes the tiers of needs that must be fulfilled for a person to achieve self-actualization. Fundraising is often linked to projects that help people meet those basic human needs. If our focus is to help those in need, we should also work to help them to feel cared for and to build their self-esteem.

It is an inherent human desire to be self-sufficient. Most people, regardless of their current struggles, would like to be independent. All projects, in the end, should work toward promoting those being served.

Endowment

In the world of philanthropy, an endowment is a pool of money that is invested, with the resulting investment income being used for a specific purpose by a charitable organization.

The existence of endowments is well established at colleges, universities, and many other nonprofit organizations. In fact, it is very common for endowments to be in place at larger organizations with a 501(c)(3) charitable not-for-profit status.

Typically, the principal of an endowment is not used to support operations; only a portion of the investment earnings are used. The principal of an

> "Self-leadership is about digging out your hidden endowment and making them known and useful to those who need it most."
>
> **Israelmore Ayivor**

endowment is intended to grow by retaining a portion of the investment earnings each year and through the addition of new contributions to the account.

Endowments usually carry a broad restriction for how they may be used by the charity. This means that the earnings generated must be used for a general area of operation by the organization as directed by the donor or donors who originally provided the gift to establish the fund. Care must be exercised in the crafting of an endowment's policy so that the restricted use is not so specific as to render it unusable in the future, if circumstances change. Therefore, it is wise for an endowment policy to give the board and the executive director some latitude for the use of the revenue it provides.

An endowment is used to provide perpetual support. We live in an unpredictable world, and in such an environment, endowments can serve as a stable source of revenue for an organization in the event of economic difficulties. Indeed, there are countless examples of organizations that have survived hard times because of their endowment.

Experts suggest that a financially healthy organization should have a year's worth of expenses in its annual reserve to manage its cash flow. However, an organization's endowment is not included as a part of the reserve, because the principal needs to remain invested and is not available to use to cover expenses.

It is not unusual for an endowment to be funded through bequests or by using gifts of highly appreciated assets. The endowments of most organizations are conservatively invested in securities, with a primary objective of generating income and a secondary objective of growth.

Because of the expertise required for the oversight of the long-term investment strategy being employed, endowments are usually managed outside of the organization by a foundation or brokerage firm.

The finance committee of the board should be charged with the fiscal oversight of the endowment, consistent with the investment policy of the organization.

Operationally, there should be stated policies to guide the board of an organization and its executive director with regard to how it plans to use the revenue provided by its endowment. The income provided by most endowments will be broadly restricted for use in a particular purpose or program.

Keeping that broad restriction in mind, the specific use of endowment revenue should be determined or reaffirmed annually by action of the organization's board of directors in consultation with the executive director. Checks and balances need to be in place to prevent the misuse or misappropriation of endowment revenue.

Some donors may have the opinion that the danger in having a large endowment is that it may allow an organization to operate with a certain amount of autonomy from its governance. That's why it is important for the board to exercise ultimate authority for the oversight and management of the endowment. The investment policy must be clear and the use of endowment revenue consistent with the intent of the donor.

Ultimately, a properly managed endowment can prove to be pivotal to the long-term financial health of an organization. On top of providing economic security, endowments also show that an organization is responsible and proactive. It is believed that donors see the existence of an organization's endowment as evidence of good stewardship. This has the positive impact of prompting them to think well of the organization and its mission.

Accountability

Accountability is a more powerful word than responsibility. To be accountable for something is to personally commit to making it happen. Bill Belichick, famed American football coach, once said: "When your teammate looks you in the eye and holds you accountable, that's the greatest kind of leadership there is."

Many people view accountability and responsibility as interchangeable words. To be accountable for something means more being responsible. It means that you personally accept the consequences, good or bad, of the outcome.

"Responsibility equals accountability equals ownership. And a sense of ownership is the most powerful weapon a team or organization can have"

Pat Summitt

For example, in the organization I worked at, I was both responsible and accountable to all the persons I worked with. It was always my responsibility to plan the weekly staff meeting agenda, send out advance reminders, and start the meeting on time. However, if for some reason I forgot about the meeting, then I was accountable to all the staff to explain what happened and then make things right. For me, it may mean more than a simple, "I am sorry."

Apologizing for not being prepared and being willing to adjust to some expectations or deadlines that were established at previous staff meetings were requirements of my job.

The line between accountability and responsibility can be confusing. It is helpful to associate accountability with the process of reporting what you did or did not accomplish to others who are impacted, as well as being prepared to accept and deal with the consequences.

Accountability, in the context of nonprofits, involves the obligation of an organization to evaluate its impact, disclose the results, and own up to its performance. On an individual level, as fundraisers, we are accountable to all stakeholders: ourselves, our coworkers, our organization's board members, our donors, and volunteers.

Accountability is a good thing, because our work holds greater significance when there are consequences, positive or negative. Steve Rothschild writes, "when people get something for nothing, they don't value it." Mutual accountability ensures that an organization's employees value what they receive from their work, which means they are more likely to fulfill their responsibility and succeed in the long run.

As nonprofit fundraisers, we are accountable for collecting funds, telling our organization's stories, and managing our resources. We are held responsible for carrying out these tasks. Moreover, we are also accountable for the mistakes we make. We are accountable for providing reports on time and for making sure all funds are accounted for. We are accountable for making sure that the results of our fundraising efforts, including those online, are transparent.

As fundraisers, we also need to hold ourselves accountable for our attitudes and behaviors. Our attitudes and behaviors should reflect those of our organization and are easily discernable by donors. Doug and Polly White (2011), management consultants, suggest that one quality of accountable employees is that they are willing to learn from their failures, while also not blaming others for their shortcomings.

Accountability has the power to change nonprofit organizations for the better. In the past, blind trust might have been enough for donors to support an organization, but in the modern fundraising world, blind trust alone is not enough to earn the support of donors.

Accountability leads nonprofit organizations to be more reflective and transparent in all aspects of the organization. Just as a government is accountable to its citizens in a democratic society, so are organizations accountable to justify its actions to its constituencies.

Section 4

Sharing Ideas and Words of Encouragement

- A Book to Assist Fundraisers
- Incentive to Write
- Concluding Thoughts

A Book to Assist Fundraisers

This book is written for anyone who is, or who might become, a fundraiser at a nonprofit. It is put together for those who believe in the idea of philanthropy, which is the belief that money, in the hands of generous individuals, can be used to do real, tangible good in the world.

If you are looking to become a fundraiser, this book will not provide you with everything you need to start a career in fundraising. What I hope is that it provides you with the current best fundraising practices, shows you what has and hasn't worked for

"It is more rewarding to watch money change the world than to watch it accumulate."

Glory Steinem

others in the field, and tells you stories of professionals who have proven themselves to be successful through adopting a personal belief in their organization's mission and purpose as motivation for their fundraising efforts. I hope that this book has instilled in you the importance of mastering the traits that enable fundraisers to love their jobs, as well as serving as a reminder to always have a mindset of trust, gratitude, and accountability.

If you are a new fundraiser, or are soon to become a fundraiser, there are opportunities available to help you learn more. In fact, there many books, articles, professional associations, and training opportunities with experts in the field of fundraising to help you become an effective fundraiser.

Even so, my experience with several of the training sessions that I attended was that they were not very inclusive in their presentation. They were designed for large, educational institutions, and all too often, nonprofit organizations are not able to afford such workshops for their staff, at least not on a regular basis. Nevertheless, there are a great many organizations, like MCC Great Lakes, that utilizes their alumni's experience as a form of staff development. Our relationship building with donors is a very different experience. I hope that the ideas provided and the experiences shared in this book can bridge that gap.

My hope for this book is that anyone, regardless of their level of fundraising experience, will benefit from the suggestions and techniques provided. For anyone working at a nonprofit, this book provides suggestions from both practitioners and scholars about how to aid in shaping your organization's mission and vision in a way that will help it improve its impact.

This book is primarily written for American nonprofit fundraisers. However, the main themes and ideas listed in this book will be easily applicable to anyone working in developing nations. Naturally, people's attitudes and expectations with regards to fundraising may change a bit from culture to culture, but it should be possible to adjust this book's teachings to work with local cultural values.

Within this book, my objective has been to provide good discussion topics for nonprofit board members, staff, and fundraisers as they develop fundraising strategies for their organization. Remember that revisiting and learning from what you have done in the past will help you and your organization to redefine and improve what you do in the future. Be willing to constantly adapt activities based on the economic environment surrounding your core community donors. Fundraisers must always exercise good judgment, which involves being aware of the current context of your donors. For example, if there has been a natural disaster or an economic recession in a place where some of your organization's donors reside, take this into account when you ask them for donations.

All fundraisers have stories of a failed project, but they also have the tools and tricks they relied on to move forward and learn from those failures. This book serves as an encouragement and an inspiration to share and affirm each other's work in fundraising. As the saying goes, we must learn from our mistakes. Indeed, but we cannot make mistakes from which to learn from if we never try new things.

The main purpose of this book is to share what I learned from my fundraising experience. For most of us at nonprofits, we learn by doing. It has been important to me to share what I have learned from other fundraisers, which is why I have included a survey of an array of fundraising professionals.

In the end, even though this book is designed to help you become more effective as a fundraiser, the single most important part of being a fundraiser is to be faithful to your organization's mission and objectives as you pursue your dreams.

Comments from survey respondents

I am happy that you have taken this project upon yourself which I believe is a worthy cause and one that will prove to be very helpful to many who are in the field as well as those who will be coming into the field in years to come.

I am certain that you will be enlisting the advice and counsel of those in the nearby Lilly School of Philanthropy as you move forward with the project. And when the manuscript is ready having the prominent ones endorsing it, would help to promote a wider distribution and use of this document which will be born out of actual field experience supported by decades of academic experience.

It was a privilege to participate in the survey from the limited experience I have had the past few years. I look forward with anticipation the publishing of the book.

Incentive to Write

The ability to write well is a gift that provides the ability to effectively communicate our thoughts and ideas. Unfortunately, writing in English—my second language—is not one of my strengths. Some say writing is an art form or a form of therapy. I certainly admire the practice, but it does not come easy for me. What I do appreciate about writing is that it has provided me with the means to continue my learning.

Some scholars write for fun or because they get paid to do so. For a good portion of my life, I only wrote because my professors told me to.

> "Motivation is what gets you started. Habits is what keeps you going."
>
> **Jim Ryun**

Funding A Mission

Thankfully, with the counsel of a few writing experts, I have come to enjoy writing and do so regularly.

As I was planning to retire from the executive director's position at MCC

Great Lakes, I was encouraged by my mentors, colleagues, and friends to write about my fundraising experiences. Considering that I, for the most part, enjoyed my years working for nonprofits and at educational institutions, I began to consider writing about my experiences.

When I look back at my career, my fundraising work was the most fulfilling and satisfying work I did. In my 33-year career, I was never as gratified or fulfilled at the end of a fiscal year as I was as a fundraiser. I can say with confidence that my inspiration to write, for the most part, came from the work I did in fundraising. I enjoyed fundraising so much because each and every day, whether I was traveling or in the office, I went to work fully believing that I was doing something good. I always felt energized and built on the momentum of the day before. I was usually well-received, and donors responded well to my stories.

My fundraising work gave me the opportunity to tackle global issues that would have otherwise been out of my reach. Through my experience at MCC Great Lakes, my staff and I were able to lead and position the organization to be in a better financial situation than when I first arrived.

Like many others in the field, I did not go to school to study fundraising. My formal on-the-job training took place when I was officially hired to work in fundraising at MCC Great Lakes. Luckily, I documented my fundraising work through the years in the form of my many journals and collections of notes. One of my professors in graduate school told his class: If you know something, put it in writing, and work hard to publish it. After all, there is a chance that some of your readers may benefit from your insight.

In addition to reporting from my personal work experience, I employed three different methods to collect the information provided in this book. These are: reviews of fundraising literature, the inclusion of quotes from books in the field of fundraising, and reflections on a series of meaningful conversations about fundraising that I had with others. Over the years, I've learned much from various workshops and by simply observing and listening to colleagues.

For me, fundraising gave me the gift of friendship. It was a joy to join other fundraisers in collecting money for the purpose providing for the needy. It was truly amazing to see so many passionate people making a difference in the lives of others. I was enriched beyond my imagination because of the opportunity I had to work at MCC.

The experience of fundraising taught me to utilize skills that I didn't even know that I possessed. I was able to work with donors who believed in doing what they could to support projects that they cared for. As a fundraiser, I worked hard to link donors to ongoing and new programs in an effort to help them make an impactful difference. All these things made the hard work of fundraising fun.

It was gratifying for me to see the level of trust donors had in MCC. Another true joy of fundraising was getting to thank donors for making so many of our success stories possible. It was clear to me that donors gave money with the pure motive of simply making a difference in the lives of others. Donors knew that the programs they supported at MCC were geared toward human development with a future goal of securing the independence of those we supported.

Concluding Thoughts

Fundraising is considered by me and others in the field as a service to others. The goal of fundraising is to secure enough funding to meet the annual fundraising target, to acquire new donors, and to maintain relationships with current donors. More than anything else, fundraising is about fulfilling the mission of your organization.

There is nothing more meaningful or rewarding than the call to work to change the lives of others. Millions of people around the globe depend on the work of nonprofit organizations to help them survive difficult situations.

> "What we have done for ourselves alone dies with us; what we have done for others and the world remains and is immortal."
>
> **Albert Pike**

Forcefully displaced people depend on us for food, shelter, safety, clothing, and even education. In many ways, fundraising is a noble profession. From my experience, whether fundraisers felt called to the profession or whether they were doing it because it was their job, fundraisers matter because they are helping to provide compassion to those who desperately need it.

All of us who have worked at nonprofit organizations dedicated to addressing peace and justice have committed ourselves to stand with those who need our support. The countless displaced citizens and refugees around the world, the homeless in our own back yards, and those who lack basic food and shelter all benefit from the work we do.

We live in a broken but fixable world. If we all work hard to combine our resources for the support and the wellbeing of others, anything is possible.

Our broken world must bring us together to work toward the common goal of alleviating the suffering of our fellow human beings. Finding the right balance between peacefully confronting conflict and, at the same time, helping those in need is what nonprofit organizations have done for centuries.

I believe nonprofit organizations and their supporters are in the best position to help

Concluding Thoughts

fix our world, as they reach out to those who are without the resources they need to help themselves.

I hope that this book helps you to find a vision or expand your horizons. I trust that the findings and data from this research will be helpful to nonprofit board members, staff, and donors.

At the end of any fiscal year, a fundraiser should be prepared to say that their organization's success was due not only to their organization's fundraising efforts but also to their organization's mission and purpose, the compassionate and caring response of its constituency, and because of the committed leadership from its board of directors. An organization should be prepared to give ample credit to local communities that support its efforts.

At Great Lakes, we exceeded our fundraising goals each and every year. This was only possible because we had a well-articulated and well-understood mission statement that effectively communicated the overall scope of what we hoped to accomplish at our organization. We also provided transparent annual financial reports to our constituency.

I hope that, at the end of the day, any fundraiser can say that what they accomplished was due to their relationship with the donor community and their wholehearted belief in their organization's mission.

Much of this book's content focuses on what a fundraiser can do to build meaningful relationships with donors. In summary, the following list comprises what I consider to be the priorities that most important for a fundraiser remember when speaking to donors:
- Be personal in your approach
- Tailor your approach to each individual donor
- Speak the truth
- Be relevant
- Listen to what the donor is telling you
- Communicate trustworthiness
- Increase the visibility of your organization's successes by telling its stories

All who work at nonprofit organizations are in the business of providing food, money, shelter, and materials to the needy around the world. And yet, if we as fundraisers don't empower those on the receiving end of aid to stand on their own feet, we will have failed them. For it is because of our compassion that we assist those who look for a second chance to improve their lives.

In the spirit of service to others, Gail Perry (2007) summarized it best: "I believe fundraising is one of the noblest and most altruistic activities a human can make. Everything we do as fundraisers is for the betterment of mankind. I wish everybody on our planet would dedicate some of their time to raising resources to make their communities and the world a better place" (p. 49).

The donors we work with today, just like those who came before them, are immersed in a culture of giving that will last for many generations to come. As Nelson Mandela wrote: "Man's goodness is a flame that can be hidden but never extinguished."

Finally, at the end of the fiscal year, when your organization's budget is balanced and you inform your board of that wonderful news, took a few moments to share a particularly poignant story that took place in the last twelve month, and now cherish the donor relationship behind that story.

Ours is a win-win game. When one year ends the slate is wiped clean and you may ask yourself, "now what?" Well, a new year is upon us. I have new goals and it is time to get busy. Pick up that phone and schedule your next donor visit!

Hebrews 6:10 (CEV)
"God is always fair. He will remember how you helped his people in the past and how you are still helping them. ..."

Bibliography

A Common Place, (Volume 24 Number 3, Summer 2018) A Publication of Mennonite Central Committee, Learning to Lead Through Relationship, (p. 4-7)

A Common Place, (Volume 25 Number 1, Winter 2019) A Publication of Mennonite Central Committee, Technical Training in India, (p.16-17)

Bateson, John. (2008) Leadership in the Nonprofit World. Published by Greenwood Publishing Group, Inc

Bary, Ilona, M. (2016) 5th, Edition. Effective Fundraising for Nonprofits: Real – World Strategies That Works. By Delta Printing Solutions, INC.

Besinger, R. Jeavons. T., (2000). Growing Givers Hearts: Treating Fundraising As a Ministry. Published by Jossey-Bass

Brinckerhoff, Peter (2012), Smart Stewardship for Nonprofits: Making the Right Decision in Good Times and Bad. Published by John Wiley & Sons, Inc. Hoboken, NJ.

Carter-Black, Alexis (2006), Getting Grants: The complete Manual of Proposal Development and Administration. By Self-Counsel Press.

Carver, John (2002) On Board Leadership. Selected Writings From The Creator of the World's Most Provocative and Systematic Governance Model. Published by Jossey - Bass

Carver, John & Carver, Mariam, (2009), A Carver Policy Governance Guide, A Policy Governance Model and the Role of the Board Members.

Carver, John & Mariam M. Carver (1997), The CEO Role Under Policy Governance. Published by Jossey-Bass The CHRONICLE of PHILANTHROPY (June 2018). The Disappearing Donor. Published by The Chronicle of Higher Education. The Chronicle of Philanthropy Monthly Magazine Publication.

Bibliography

De Pree, Max, (1997). Leading without Power: Finding Hope in Serving Community. By Jossey-Bass

Gifford, L. Gayle, (2005) How we are Doing? A 1-Hour Guide to Evaluating Your Performance as a Nonprofit Board. Published by Emerson & Church.

Ebener, R. Dan, (2012), Leadership Wisdom from the Beatitudes: Blessings for Leaders. Liturgical Press.

G. William Domhoff, Who Roles America: Wealth, Income and Power (2010) Published by McGraw Hill Higher Education.

Grace, Bill, (1999) The Spiritual of leadership. Published by Center for Ethical leadership. This book among other important spiritual behaviors, it highlights, courage, transformational leadership.

Handy, Femida & Konsrath Sara. (November 2017), On Line Blog *"Conversation) also see (http://www.ypin.org)* - Five reasons why people give.

Henri Nouwen – (2011) A Spirituality of Fundraising Upper room Publisher

Kachinske, E. & Kachinske, T. (2011), Nonprofit Data Quality: Maintaining Good Data in A Not-for-Profit Environment.

Kanter, Beth. Sherman, Aliza; (2017.) The Happy Healthy Nonprofit, Published by John Wiley & Sons, Inc, Hoboken, New Jersey.

Kouzes M. James and Posner Z. Barry (1995). The Leadership Challenge: How to Keep Getting Extraordinary Things Done in Organizations. Published by Jossey-Bass

Light, Paul C. (2000), Making Nonprofit Work: A report on the Tides of Nonprofit Management Reform. Published by Brookings Institution Press.

Lill, J. David & Lill, K. Jennifer & (2015), Cause Selling: A Guide to Successful Nonprofit Fundraising: the Sanford Way. DM Bass Publication

Martin W. Sandler & Deborah A. Hudson (1998) Beyond The Bottom Line: How To Do More With Less in Nonprofit and Public Organizations. Oxford University Press

Masaoka, Jan, (2011), The nonprofit's Guide to Human Resources: Managing Your Employees and Volunteers. Bang Printing.

Maloney, Deirdre (2012) The Mission Myth: Building nonprofit momentum through better business. Published by Business Solution, San Diego, CA

McLaughlin A. Thomas (2001) Trade Secrets for Nonprofit Managers. Published by John Wiley and Sons, Inc.

McNott, Marshall, (2008) nonprofit Nonsense & Common Sense. Robert D. Reed Publisher.

Mennonite World Review (June 2018) (*Refugees come for the aid, stay for the love. pp. 13)* An independent Ministry of Christian journalism serving Mennonites and the global Anabaptist Movement, Published Biweekly by Mennonite World Review Inc.

Munday T. Terry (2009) *It's Not About The Money:* How to tap into God-Given generosity.

National University, Stanford Institute of Philanthropy John F. Kennedy University. A weekly email funding news and analysis report. (June 2018)

Palmer, J. Parker, (2000), Let Your Life Speak, Jossey – Bass Inc., Publisher.

Palmer, J. Parker, (2004), A Hidden Wholeness: The Journey Toward An Undivided Life. Published by Jossy-Bass

Pakroo, H. Peri, (2013) Starting & Building a Nonprofit: A Practical Guide, Bang Printing, 2005. www.Nolo.com

Perry, Gail, (2007) Fired-Up, Turn Board Passion into Acton. By John Wiley & Sons, Inc.

Rothschild, Steve, (2012) The Non Nonprofit, For-Profit Thinking for nonprofit Success. Publish by Jossey-Bass

Stanford, Sean –Stockton, Why People Really Give to Charity.

Stanford Social Innovation Review June 25, 2008

Teitel, Martin, (2012) Winning Foundation Grants: A Foundation CEO Reveals the Secrets You Need to Know. Emerson and Church Publishers.

Wallace, Nicole. (Editor), The Chronicle of philanthropy, the disappearing donor, (June 2018, pp 9-52,), A publication of chronicle of Higher education monthly magazine.

Watters, Joe, (1967), Fundraising with Business: 40 New Strategies for Nonprofit. By John Wiley & Sons, INC.

White R.J. Karen, Practical Project Management for Agile Nonprofit (2013). Marvin House Press

White, Doug & Polly, (2011) Let Go to Grow: Why Some Businesses Thrive and Others Fail to Reach Their Potential. Published by Palari Publishing

Wolf, Thomas (2011), How to Connect with Donors and Double the Money you Raise. Published by Emerson and Church.

Other Sources I Consulted and Recommendations for Future Readings:

I recommend the Association of Fundraising Professional of Fundraising Course Participant Manual (2010, or the latest edition you can get your hands on). This manual provides you, among other useful materials, with an overview of fundraising principles.

It is recommended that all nonprofit professionals read this publication. It provides you with the latest news and fresh ideas about fundraising, in addition to some commentary and resources to help you meet your fundraising efforts

For those from faith-based organizations, there are many good examples of Biblical sources on giving. Here are a couple that are familiar to many. Second Corinthians 9:7 – "Each of you should give what you have decided in your heart to give, not resultantly or under compulsion, for God loves a cheerful giver."

Gail Perry is an international fundraising consultant and an expert in nonprofit philanthropic with over thirty years' experience. You will find video-based instruction from Gail. Search for "Firedup Fundraising Blog" from Gail Perry.

Rebekah B. Basinger (200), A good resource book for fundraisers. After all the staff read her book *Growing Givers' Hearts Treating Fundraising as a Ministry*, I invited Basinger to act as a consultant to the MCC Great Lakes Office so that staff could spend a couple of days learning from Basinger's wisdom and experiences.

The Chronicle of Philanthropy: a monthly magazine. It has the latest national trends and tips on fundraising, forecasts, and best practices. For me, this magazine was on my "to read" list every month and I passed it on to my fundraising team members.

The magazine reports research projects of the nation's largest nonprofit individuals who give the most money to nonprofit groups each year.

Credit Suisse Global Wealth Report of 2018.

The Credit Suisse Research Institute's Global Wealth Report is the most comprehensive source of global household wealth information. It reports an aggregate global wealth as well

Other Sources I Consulted and Recommendations for Future Readings:

as analyzing wealth held by 5.0 billion adults across the globe, from the least affluent to the wealthiest individuals.

You can download this information for interesting facts and figures. https:www.credit-suisse.com

Appendix A

Survey Findings Report

In order to support the very premise of the book—that funding a mission really does matter—a survey was conducted. All nonprofit fundraising professionals in the study were contacted by phone asking them to participate in the study, followed by email with brief description of the purpose of the study, a timeline and an assurance to the participants of total confidentiality.

Sixteen survey participants received 24 questions by email. We garnered a 100% response. In addition, we received 15 written comments. Not everyone that completed the survey provided written comments, and several offered more than one comment.

It is important to note that the sample size for this survey might be too small to draw any significant conclusions. However, the importance of the findings is that it provides a snapshot from the perspective of individuals working in three different types of nonprofit organizations, each of which has its set of challenges and opportunities. Participants also represent domestic and international work.

This report has two parts: First, the responses to the 24-question survey, and second, a thematic description of the written comments.

As I promised to survey participants, findings are shared in aggregate. However, I took the liberty to add comments of clarity to three areas— "<u>Commitment to Mission,</u>" "<u>Why Donors Give</u>", and "<u>Quality and Measurement of Success</u>" —and imbedded them in the text. This is in addition to survey responses attached in Appendix B.

Appendix A

Findings & Analysis
N=16

Questionnaires were sent out—see Appendix A—to 16 different persons currently identified as fundraisers representing different nonprofit organizations in the following areas:

Organizations Represented in the Study:
- **38 percent** Educational Organizations
- **31 percent** Health and Human Services
- **31 percent** Relief and Development

Gender of Respondents
- **44 percent** Female
- **56 percent** Male

Titles:
- **19 percent** Director of Development/Advancement
- **19 percent** VP for Development

- **6 %** Director of Fundraising
- **38 percent** Executive Director (CEO)
- **18 percent** Other Titles (Special Assistant, Chief Development Officer and Interim VP)

1. **Are you the contact person for fundraising at your organization or institution?**

Response
- **63 percent** said yes they are
- **31 percent** responded no they are not
- **6%** no response

2. **Indicate how you gained your expertise in fundraising. Please check all that apply.**

Response
- **75 percent** of the respondents indicated gaining expertise by both ...a combination of training and on-the-job
- **19 percent** No one learned fundraising by attending training alone.
- **6%** On-the-job training

3. **Does your organization have a written statement with objectives to provide guidance in fundraising?**

Response
- **69 *percent*** of participants admitted to having a statement with written objectives
- ***31 percent*** said they do not have one.

4. **Do you believe your organization's mission statement is clearly understood by your stakeholders and your constituents? Please check only one.**

Response
- ***75 percent*** said they do
- ***13 percent*** responded by saying that their needs to be further improvements to achieve greater clarity
- ***6%*** said they do not

5. **Do you believe your fundraising work has the support of the entire staff at your organization? Please check only one.**

Response
- ***31*** percent believe *there is* **support**
- ***63 percent*** believe there is ***somewhat support***
- ***6%*** did not respond to this question

6. **Do you currently have a strategic plan to help you fundraise? Please check only one.**

<u>*Response*</u>
- ***82 percent*** said they do
- ***6%*** say they have no plan
- ***6%*** said they are working on developing one.

7. **Do you utilize your fundraising strategic goals to help measure your achievements at the end of a budget period? Please check only one.**

<u>*Response*</u>
- ***44 percent*** said they do
- ***32 percent*** said they do measure but not consistently
- ***19 percent*** said that they do not measure their achievements.

8. **How do you measure your success as a fundraiser? Please rank 1-10 points to signify importance. (1 as low and 10 as high; points from respondents are tallied up)**

<u>*Response*</u>
- ***130 points***: When ethical standards are not compromised, but rather reinforced

- ***127 points***: When my values on compassion, care, and social justice are affirmed
- ***118 points***: When ethical standards are not compromised and when effectively telling stories about work to donors

9. **Do you engage your board members in your organization's fundraising efforts? Please check one.**

Response
- ***13 percent*** are fully engaged in their fundraising efforts.
- ***56 percent*** of board members are intermittently engaged.
- ***31 percent*** said their board members are not fully engaged in fundraising efforts at their organization they serve at.

10. **Please rate your board's participation (not asking for amounts) in giving to the organization. Please check only one.**

Funding A Mission

Response
- **44 percent** of their board members are participating 100 percent.
- **18 percent** of board participating in giving to their organization at 50 percent and
- **18 percent** board members participating in giving less than 50 percent

11. Please rate your staff's participation (not asking for amounts) in giving to your organization. Please check only one.

Response
- **26 percent** of staff participate all the time
- **25 percent** of staff participate more than 50% of the time but less than 100%
- **38 percent** of staff participate less than 50 percent of the time
- **18 percent** of staff had 0% participation

12. How important is listening to your donors by your entire fundraising team? Please check only one.

Response
- **63 percent** indicated extremely important
- **26 percent** indicated very important
- **6%** indicated important

13. **How well do you treat first time donors? Please check only one.**

Response
- **18 percent** said extremely well
- **25 percent** said very well
- **31 percent** said well
- **18 percent** responded somewhat well
- **6%** said not very well.

14. **How do you let your donors know that they are appreciated for their contributions?**

Response
- **44 percent** said they send hand written notes
- **44 percent** said they invite donors to come to an upcoming event
- **38 percent** said they ask their board members to write a note or call them
- **25 percent** said they call donors on the phone if a number is available

15. Why do you think donors generally give? Please rank 1-10, 1 the least important and 10 the most important reason; points from participants are tallied up.)

Response
- **128 points**: Donors give to make a difference in someone's life
- **120 points**: Donors are convinced by your mission
- **87 points**: When at least 65 percent of your funds goes to programs
- **83 points**: Donors give to benefit from tax deduction

16. Do you have a donor retention strategy developed for your organization?

Response
- **63 percent** said they do
- **31 percent** said they do not
- **6%** stated that they are in the process of developing one

17. How important is it to you and your team to pay attention to the needs of those being served by your organization? Please check only one.

Response

When asked about the value they paced on the importance or paying attention of those they serve, out of the six options provided to them, respondents allocated their answers only between extremely important and very important:

- *50 percent* stated it is *extremely important* to them that they pay attention to those they serve
- *50 percent* also stated that paying attention those they serve is *very important*

18. How important is Story Telling as part of your fundraising strategy? Please check only one.

Response
- *50 percent* extremely important
- *31 percent* very important
- *13 percent* important

19. Do you have an annual fundraising plan for your organization? Please Check only one.

Response
- **82 percent** stated they do have an annual fundraising plan
- **6%** stated as not having one, but raising fund as necessary
- **6%** said they are in the process of developing one.
- **6%** did not respond

20. **Do you have a specific revenue amount to raise in your current fundraising plan?**

Response
- **88 percent** said they do have one
- **6%** responded by indicating that revenue goals are not identified in their funding plans.
- **6%** did not respond

21. **Has your organization established an endowment to support its ongoing mission? Please check all that apply.**

Response
- **63 percent** said they do have one
- **18 percent** said that establishing endowment is part of their future plans
- **13 percent** said that they are not planning to establish an endowment anytime in the near future.

- **6%** stated as not having one

22. **Who in your organization is responsible for the overall spending of your endowment? Please check only one.**

Response
- **56 percent** indicated to be the board in consultation with the CEO
- **12 percent** said their board of directors do have the responsibility
- **12 percent** stated the CEO
- **19 percent** responded "other"

23. **How well do you utilize volunteers (not including board members) in your fundraising efforts? Please check only one.**

Response
- **12 percent** said they have utilized volunteers *extremely well*
- **12 percent** stated that they have utilized volunteers *very well*
- **19 percent** said they have utilized volunteers *well* and
- **19 percent** stated utilizing volunteers *somewhat well.*
- **25 percent** *not very well*
- **13 percent** *not extremely well*

24. How would you rate your level of satisfaction in your role as a fundraiser? Please rate your satisfaction using the scales provided and the qualitative indicators associated with the scales. Please check only one.

Response

When respondents were asked to rate their level of satisfaction of their role as fundraisers by placing themselves on the scale, their level of satisfaction of work was observed in the following rating scale.

- **13 percent** *least satisfied* on the scale between 1 and 4.
- **50 percent** *moderately satisfied* on the scale between 5-7.
- **37 percent** *very satisfied* on a scale between 8-10

Themes Gathered from Survey Participants Additional Comments

- My role in fundraising emerged out of necessity, not for pay or compensation
- Thanking donors is an essential part of donor cultivation
- Formal training in fundraising was not part of my initial introduction to the work
- Fundraising goals are and should be part of an organization's strategic goals
- Having a clear and concise mission statement is key to fundraising
- Marketing is an essential tool and strategy in communicating mission
- It is important to have a culture of philanthropy embedded in an organization so that the responsibility of fundraising is shared by everyone
- Important to connect donors to the organization and not to the staff
- Fundraising is a way of carrying out ministry
- Board engagement is critical to successful fundraising

Notes of the Additional Comments Provided by Survey Participants

Reference to Question 1:

#1. Yes, but all of our development officers are "contact" people. We are all always on the lookout for ways to advance the mission of the organization, so anyone can become a conduit through which donors connect. I am simply the person who coordinates all of our development activity.

Reference to Question 2: (Several comments)

#2. I began learning about fundraising while serving on boards and when I accepted my current development job, I began a more formal training program.

#2. I can't tell you how much I appreciate what you are attempting to do by documenting your experience in fundraising. It is time for us to do what we do well by listening and learning sometimes from one another. This is one way to keep learning. I have been in sessions with some high powered and highly paid consultant who simply told us what we already know. I hope you can tell some of your fundraising stories.

Appendix A

Reference to Question 4:

#4. Our mission statement is key to connecting to our constituents and donors. We have a specific marketing piece that allows us to clearly communicate our mission statement and create interest from donors and potential donors.

Historically, we have had 100% participation from our board of directors and >90% participation from employees. Alumni participation averages 28% which is above average among our peer schools.

We have sought to cultivate a culture of philanthropy among employees so that they are aware of advancement opportunities when they are engaging in other ways with our constituents.

Reference to Question 6: (Several comments)

 # 6. We had a strategic plan that includes fundraising goals. The goals are more clearly defined in a strategy meeting of our development council each August. We adjust our strategy throughout the year depending on how we are meeting our goals.

#6. We had one, but never looked at it. I think we need one that we can all use and works. On the flip side, for now, we are doing fine in our fundraising, so why do we need it?

#6. Thank you for including me in your research. It is a privilege working with you on this project. I hope your work will produce less academic, with a touch of hands on, everyday work experience report.

Reference to Question 8:

#8. There are times when I am challenged to relate to people who do not hold the exact same personal values that I do, but my job is to connect the donor to the organization, not to build the relationship only with me.

Reference to Question 9: (Several comments)

9. We are working on this. Our board members, over the past 5 years, have become more involved with fundraising.

#9. Some of our board members are engaged fully by giving their time, resource and I appreciate what they stand for. However, others are there simply for the experience. You can tell they are new at this for sure, they do respect what we do and yet they do not have much wisdom to offer.

Reference to Question 23:

#23. We are very staff-driven in our fundraising. In the past, capital campaigns have had a volunteer steering committee, but we have not utilized a committee for about 12 years.

Reference to Question 24:
(Several Comments)

#24. Fundraising is ministry. It takes drive and courage to do the work, but it takes a pastoral care and sensitivity to do it well with donors. I recommend the little book *The Spirituality of Fundraising* by Henri Nouwen as a resource. I require my staff to read through it every year.

24. I am not a regular or professional fund raiser. I began 21 years ago as a CEO because of necessity, continued throughout the 21 years as a volunteer on top of my regular duties, and now in my "retired" time. I have never been paid a cent for my services. I have been involved with other volunteers also not paid. Together we must have raised more than six or seven million dollars for the organization. I have lost count. That gives us a sense of satisfaction that money cannot buy. But I am getting very tired.

#24. I write a personal thank you on the letter if they are reoccurring donors or have given a specific amount

#24. I am happy that you have taken this project upon yourself which I believe is a worthy cause and one that will prove to be very helpful to many who are in the field as well as those who will be coming into the field in years to come.

Appendix A

I am certain that you will be enlisting the advice and counsel of those in the nearby Lilly School of Philanthropy as you move forward with the project. And when the manuscript is ready having the prominent ones endorsing it, would help to promote a wider distribution and use of this document which will be born out of actual field experience supported by decades of academic experience.

It was a privilege to participate in the survey from the limited experience I have had the past few years. I look forward with anticipation the publishing of the book.

Appendix B

FUNDING A MISSION SURVEY: MAY, 2018

This survey questionnaire is designed to augment the research within the fundraising book **_Funding A Mission_**. Data is being gathered from approximately 16 different not-for-profit professionals with fundraising experience both in the United States and in other parts of the world.

Please respond to the following **24 questions** and send your response as soon as possible. This is 100 % anonymous, and you or your organization will not be identified in anyway in this publication. Only data received will be analyzed and reported. The findings from the survey will be shared with you as soon as the analysis is completed.

QUESTIONS

*Please indicate your current position by selecting the most appropriate role you are engaged in at your organization:

____Director of Development/Advancement
____VP for Development/Advancement
____Director of Fundraising
____Executive Director (CEO) with some responsibility for fundraising
Other. _____

1. Are you the contact person for fundraising at your organization or institution?
___Yes
___ No
Comment _____

2. Indicate how you gained your expertise in fundraising. Please check all that apply.
____I learned by attending training classes
____I learned by on-the-job training
___Both
Comments _____

3. Does your organization have a written statement with objectives to provide guidance in fundraising?
___Yes
___No
Comment _____

4. Do you believe your organization's mission statement is clearly understood by your stakeholders and your constituents? Please check only one.

___Yes, it is clearly understood
___No, it is not clearly understood
___Need further improvement to achieve greater clarity

5. Do you believe your fundraising work has the support of the entire staff at your organization? Please check only one.

___ Yes
___ No
___ Somewhat
Comment _____

6. Do you currently have a strategic plan to help you fundraise? Please check only one.

___ Yes
___ No
___ We are working on a new strategic plan
Comment _____

7. Do you utilize your fundraising strategic goals to help measure your achievements at the end of a budget period? Please check only one.

___ Yes, our fundraising results are measured based on our strategic goals
___ No, our fundraising results are not measured based on our strategic goals
___ We do not consistently use our strategic goals to measure our performance

8. How do you measure your success as a fundraiser? Please rank 1-10 to signify importance. (1 as low and 10 as high.)

___ My overall happiness and excitement about the job
___ My ethical standards are not compromised but rather they are reinforced
___ I am effectively telling stories about my work to our donors
___ My values on compassion, care, and social justice are affirmed

9. Do you engage your board members in your organization's fundraising efforts? Please check one.

___ Yes, our board members are fully engaged in our fundraising efforts
___ No, our board members are not fully engaged in fundraising efforts
___ Board members are intermittently engaged
Comment_____

Appendix B

10. Please rate your board's participation (not asking for amounts) in giving to the organization. Please check only one.

___ 100 percent participation in giving and getting for the organization
___ Above 50% participation but less than 100%
___ Less than 50%
___ 0% participation
___ I don't know
Comment_____

11. Please rate your staff's participation (not asking for amounts) in giving to your organization. Please check only one.

___ 100% participation in giving and getting for the organization
___ Above 50% participation but less than 100%
___ Less than 50%
___ 0% participation
___ I don't know
Comment_____

12. How important is listening to your donors by your entire fundraising team? Please check only one.

___ Extremely important
___ Very important

Funding A Mission

___ Important
___ Somewhat important
___ Not very important
___ Not extremely important

13. How well do you treat first time donors? Please check only one.

___ Extremely well
___ Very well
___ Well
___ Somewhat well
___ Not very well
___ Not extremely well
Comment_____

14. How do you let your donors know that they are appreciated for their contributions?

___ Send a hand written thank you letter
___ Call the donor if a phone number is available
___ Ask a board member to write a note or call
___ Invite the donor to an upcoming event
___ All of the above
Comment_____

15. Why do you think donors generally give? Please rank 1-10, 1 the least important and 10 the most important reason)

___Your mission is compelling
___ Your overhead ratio appeals to them (e.g. 65% of your   funds go to programs.)
___ Donors give to make a difference in someone's life
___ Donors give due to the benefits of tax deductions

16. Do you have a donor retention strategy developed for your organization?

___ Yes we do
___ No we don't
___ We are developing one

17. How important is it to you and your team to pay attention to the needs of those being served by your organization? Please check only one.

___ Extremely Important
___ Very Important
___ Important
___ Somewhat important
___ Not very important
___ Not extremely important
Comment _____

18. How important is Story Telling as part of your fundraising strategy? Please check only one.

___ Extremely important
___ Very important
___ Important
___ Somewhat important
___ Not very important
___ Not extremely important

19. Do you have an annual fundraising plan for your organization? Please Check only one.

___ Yes, and we always know what is expected to raise for a given year
___ No, we just raise funds as necessary
___ We are developing one

20. Do you have a specific revenue amount to raise in your current fundraising plan?

___ Yes, the revenue goals are identified in our fundraising plan
___ No, the revenue goals are not identified in our fundraising plan

21. Has your organization established an endowment to support its ongoing mission? Please check all that apply.

___ Yes, we have established an Endowment
___ No, we do not have an Endowment
___ Establishing an endowment is part of our future plan
___ We are not planning to establish an endowment anytime in the near future
Comment _____

22. Who in your organization is responsible for overall spending of your endowment? Please check only one.

___ Board of Directors
___ The CEO
___ The Board of Directors in consultation with the CEO or vice versa
___ Other

23. How well do you utilize volunteers (not including board members) in your fundraising efforts? Please check only one.

___ Extremely well   ___ Somewhat well
___ Very well   ___ Not very well
___ Well   ___ Not extremely well
Comment_____

24. How would you rate your level of satisfaction in your role as a fundraiser? Please rate your satisfaction using the scales provided and the qualitative indicators associated with the scales. Please check only one.

___ Between 1-4 (Least Satisfied)
___ Between 5-7 (Moderately Satisfied)
___ Between 8-10 (Very Satisfied)

SUMMARY COMMENTS AND SUGGESTIONS: (Please write any additional comments or suggestions you may have, other questions you thought might be pertinent to the study, as well as any resource materials you would recommend. THANK YOU

PLEASE RETURN THE SURVEY TO THE FOLLOWING E-MAIL ADDRESS: zenebea8@gmail.com

Index

A

academia **viii**, 63
accountability **iii**, **xiii**, 63, **143**, **144**, **145**, 150
Accountability **143**, **144**, **145**, 146
assessment **59**, **60**, **62**, **63**, **64**
Association of Fundraising Professionals **xiii**, 55

B

benchmarks **62**, **63**, **71**, **72**, **73**
bequests **xii**
board **5**, **iii**, **xii**, **11**, **59**, **60**, **61**, **63**, **64**, **76**, **81**, **82**, **83**, **84**, **114**, **144**, **151**, **163**, **165**, **185**, **186**, **187**, **191**, **195**, **196**, **197**, **204**, **205**, **206**, **209**
Board **xii**, **57**, **81**, **82**, **83**, **168**, **169**, **172**, **193**, **204**, **209**
budget **13**, **74**, **165**, **184**, **203**

C

CEO **xvii**, **78**, **168**, **172**, **182**, **191**, **198**, **202**, **209**, **215**
Church **169**, **172**, **173**
collaboration **54**
communicate **i**, **53**, **54**, **71**, **89**, **195**
communication **xi**, **59**, **76**, **82**
Communication **xi**, **119**

D

Deirdre Maloney **73**
dependency **xiii**
development **5**, **60**, **194**, **195**, **215**
director **5**, **vi**, **xv**, **xvii**, **60**, **61**, **63**, **72**, **76**, **81**, **216**
donor base **113**

E

education **54**, **60**, **162**, **173**, **215**, **216**
Education **xiv**, **168**, **169**

educational institutions **150**
Endowment **119**, **209**
ethical **76**, **79**, **184**, **185**, **204**

F

financial **x**, **xi**, **xiii**, **xvi**, **62**, **63**, **73**, **82**, **116**, **163**
First-Time Donors **113**
fundraising plan **189**, **190**, **208**
fundraising strategy **189**, **208**

G

Gail Perry **83**, **164**, **176**
generous donors **82**
giving **xii**, **82**, **165**, **175**, **185**, **186**, **197**, **205**
goals **53**, **54**, **55**, **60**, **62**, **63**, **64**, **72**, **73**, **74**, **78**, **163**, **165**, **184**, **190**, **193**, **195**, **203**, **204**, **208**
good judgment **152**
Gratitude **115**
Guiding Principles **1**

H

Henri Nouwen **169**, **197**
Historical Context **1**

I

independence **xiii**

J

Jeffery Haguewood **74**

L

leader **xvii**, **54**, **89**
leadership **ix**, **63**, **76**, **143**, **163**, **169**

M

Max De Pree **72**
MCC; MCC Great lakes Region **5**, **ix**, **xi**, **xv**, **xvii**, **xviii**, **56**, **60**, **64**, **150**, **163**, **176**
measurement **59**, **60**, **64**, **72**, **73**, **74**, **75**
member **114**, **206**
methodology **81**
mission; mission statement **ii**, **iv**, **vii**, **viii**, **ix**, **x**, **xi**, **xvii**, **11**, **12**, **53**, **54**, **55**, **61**, **71**, **72**, **73**, **74**, **75**, **78**, **150**, **151**, **161**, **163**, **164**, **179**, **183**, **188**, **190**, **193**, **194**, **195**, **203**, **207**, **209**
Mission **vii**, **viii**, **ix**, **1**, **171**, **180**, **201**
money **xvi**, **56**, **72**, **74**, **75**, **78**, **114**, **116**, **149**, **164**, **176**, **198**

N

nonprofit **ii**, **iii**, **ix**, **xv**, **3**, **4**, **5**, **7**, **8**, **11**, **12**, **17**, **19**, **20**, **30**, **39**, **53**,

Index

54, 56, 82, 98, 122, 134, 144, 145

O

on-the-job 182, 202
On-the-job Training 1
outcome 56, 72, 143

P

Partners 1, 53
partnership 53, 54, 56
partnerships 53, 55, 56
philanthropy i, iii, v, vi, vii, ix, xi, xii, xiv, xvi, xvii, 53, 149, 173, 193, 195
potential donor 89, 90, 114
Preparedness 1

R

relationship viii, ix, xiii, 114, 117, 150, 163, 165, 196
relationships ii, xvii, xviii, 55, 161, 164
resources ii, xi, xvi, 12, 59, 62, 73, 145, 162, 163, 165, 175
response ii, 116, 163, 179, 182, 201

S

self-sufficiency xiii
skills vi, xiii, 55, 82
Solomon Belette xiv

staff vi, x, xvi, 11, 54, 59, 60, 61, 63, 64, 72, 76, 114, 118, 144, 150, 151, 163, 176, 183, 186, 193, 197, 203, 205
stakeholders x, xiii, 13, 61, 63, 73, 144, 183, 203
Steven Rothschild 73
stories 5, i, ii, iii, iv, xv, xvi, 13, 76, 145, 150, 164, 185, 194, 204
story 115, 117, 165
Strategic Planning xi, 57
strategies 62, 151
support ii, v, xi, xiv, xvi, xvii, xviii, 12, 13, 53, 56, 71, 73, 76, 82, 84, 117, 146, 162, 163, 179, 183, 190, 203, 209
survey i, ii, iii, iv, v, 60, 78, 118, 179, 180, 199, 201
sustainable xi
SWOT analysis 61

T

team 61, 62, 63, 64, 65, 176, 186, 188, 205, 207
timeline ii, 61, 64, 72, 74, 76, 179
trust iv, xi, xv, xviii, 12, 146, 150, 163

U

United States **x**, **201**
university **v**

V

volunteers **x**, **xi**, **54**, **55**, **56**, **78**, **144**, **191**, **198**, **209**

W

Wealth **1**, **35**, **169**, **176**
workshops **150**

About the Author

Zenebe Abebe, Ph.D. is the author of a newly released Autobiography *"A Long Way From Ethiopia: A Journey Fueled by Fortitude, Optimism and Resilience"*, (2018 second edition) Publish by AuthorHouse.

Zenebe Abebe's career encompasses the field of higher education. He served at four different faith-based, nonprofit liberal arts College/Universities as a dean, director, vice presidents and a professor for a total of 32 years. He also served as Executive Director (CEO) of Mennonite Central Committee of the Great Lakes Region for over 5 years.

While in higher education, among other awards, he received the Fulbright award from Fulbright Commission in Bonn, Germany and the J. William Fulbright Foreign Scholarship Board in Washington DC.

He has authored numerous academic articles in the areas of global education, conflict resolution, race relations and equity and inclusion in higher education as well as writing book reviews and book chapters.

Zenebe, holds a Ph.D., M.S., B.A., and A.A. degrees.

To contact the author, write zenebea8@gmail.com

www.ingramcontent.com/pod-product-compliance
Ingram Content Group UK Ltd.
Pitfield, Milton Keynes, MK11 3LW, UK
UKHW022214230426
12048UKWH00016BA/839